GINSPIRATION

Penguin
Random
House

Designed by Vanessa Hamilton
Compiled and edited by Libby Brown
Jacket Designer Vanessa Hamilton
Text (pp96-141) Klaus St. Rainer
Photography (pp96-141) Armin Smailovic

Special Sales Creative Project Manager
Alison Donovan
Pre-Production Producer
Rebecca Fallowfield
Senior Producer Charlotte Oliver

Material previously published in *Craft Spirits*
(2016) and *Cocktails* (2016)
by Dorling Kindersley Limited
80 Strand, London WC2R 0RL

Copyright © 2014, 2017
Dorling Kindersley Limited
A Penguin Random House Company

6 8 10 9 7 5

005 – 309573 – Nov/2017

A CIP catalogue record for this book
is available from the British Library.

ISBN 978-0-2413-3255-9

Printed and bound in China

A WORLD OF IDEAS
SEE ALL THERE IS TO KNOW

www.dk.com

Contents

Gin is the most **full-flavoured** of all clear spirits. Basically a neutral vodka that is distilled with flavours, it has a **distinctive** taste that comes predominantly from traditional botanicals, such as juniper berries, citrus peel, and coriander. The first form of gin was called **jenever**, which can be traced back to sixteenth- or seventeenth-century Holland. Perfect with tonic water, the world's favourite type of gin is **London dry** – this **juniper-heavy** variety lacks sugar and is usually higher in alcohol than other gins. Innovative craft producers use **new distilling** techniques and go to great lengths to source the most complex **botanicals** available. Explore the diversity of gin, then let your **creative juices** flow.

And so it Be-GINs...

Every spirit starts with a raw ingredient that goes through several stages of transformation. The main stages are fermenting, in which the alcohol is created, and distilling, in which this alcohol is separated and condensed in myriad ways to create a spirit.

Preparing

Distilled spirits are produced from an array of raw materials, including grapes, potatoes, and grains (see pp8–9). Depending on the spirit and the technique, producers may grind the raw material into a coarse meal to break it down and release starch, which converts into sugars. Alternatively, non-grain materials, such as potatoes, sugar cane, and fruits, are cooked or juiced. The resultant sugars are then mixed with pure water and cooked to produce a mash, before being transferred to the mash "tun" – the fermenting container.

Fermenting

Once producers have prepared the mash, it is ready for fermentation, which is a natural process of decomposition. Producers need to add yeast for fermentation to occur – yeast feeds on the sugar in the prepared mash, in the process producing alcohol and carbon dioxide (CO_2). Processes vary from producer to producer, and from spirit to spirit; some producers allow natural fermentation to occur, usually in open containers, while others use scientifically controlled methods. Fermentation can take anywhere from a few hours to several weeks, with the end product resembling a low-alcohol liquid that is similar to wine or beer – known as the "wash".

1 **Producers select** their base ingredients according to the spirit they are producing, and their preference

2 **Producers prepare** the base ingredients in different ways, including grinding and/or cooking them to form a mash

3 **Producers add yeast** to the mash in the tun so that it ferments to produce a low-proof wash

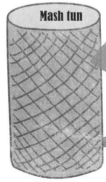

Mash tun

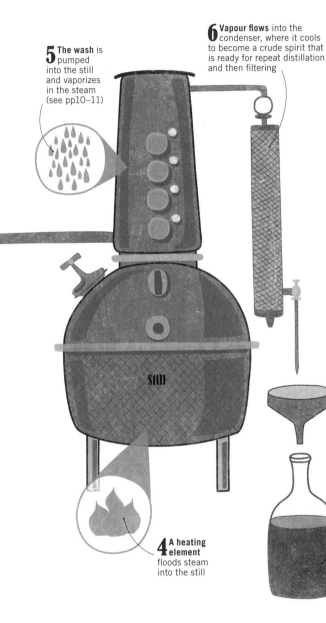

5 **The wash** is pumped into the still and vaporizes in the steam (see pp10–11)

6 **Vapour flows** into the condenser, where it cools to become a crude spirit that is ready for repeat distillation and then filtering

Still

4 **A heating element** floods steam into the still

7 **The filtered** spirit is ready for bottling, or blending and ageing

Distilling

In basic distillation, a liquid made of two or more parts is separated with the addition and subtraction of heat. The fermented alcoholic wash is heated to boiling point in a still. Elements of the wash vaporize and condense at various temperatures – the distiller selectively extracts these vapours to create a new mixture that can be bottled, or manipulated further with filtering, blending, ageing, or flavouring. This basic procedure is the same around the world for most spirits – but different stills function in different ways (see pp10–11).

Filtering

After several distillations, spirits undergo a basic filtration to eliminate large particles and sediment. Most spirits also pass through charcoal or carbon filters in order to achieve purity and flavour. Some distillers eschew this step to retain "congeners" – elements such as by-product alcohols and tannins that can lend additional character and flavour to a spirit. After filtering, the spirit may be bottled, blended, or aged.

As with any food or drink, the quality of a spirit is dependent on the quality of its base ingredients. These ingredients often appear clearly on a bottle's label, as many craft producers are keen to emphasize their fresh, local, and sustainable choices. Here is a selection of ingredients that form the foundation of many spirits, including gin.

Barley

Barley is a resilient grain with more protein and fibre than the likes of wheat and rye. It is also the best-suited grain for malting, and is therefore a key component in whisky, especially Scotch. While producers often use barley to give body to a clear spirit, it is not as commonly used as other grains due to its strong flavour.

Barley is sometimes malted (sprouted then dried) to gain more flavour and help convert its starch to sugar

Wheat

Due to their strong and nutty flavour, wheat-based spirits are not always the most popular, especially as growing numbers of people suffer from gluten intolerances. However, many distillers opt to add a little wheat to their recipes in order to impart a slight sweetness and a bread-dough aroma, and are keen to distinguish the kind they use, such as spring or winter wheat.

Wheat is milled to remove the the outer husks (bran) before it is added to the mash tun

Potato

Notoriously difficult to use in distilling, potatoes are highly perishable and release more impurities than most ingredients. However, full-bodied potato-based vodkas are flooding the market, and are popular because of their creamy mouthfeel. More so than most components, potatoes convey a true sense of place – the different varieties producers use offer a direct reflection of varying terrain and climate.

Potatoes are boiled and crushed into a purée or "soup" in order to break down their starch enough to ferment

Fruits

Although they are best known for their use in wine and cider, grapes, apples, and pears form the base of many craft spirits. Natural sugars from fruit impart a clear sweetness into spirits such as brandy, Armagnac, Calvados, and pisco. Small producers are creating spirits that evoke the remote farms, rolling hills, and bucolic countryside from where so many of these fruits are harvested.

Williams (aka Bartlett) pears are the most commonly used variety

BOTANICALS

Gin is essentially vodka that has been distilled with botanicals to impart flavour and aroma. Classic botanicals, such as juniper berries, wormwood (the key component of absinthe), and coriander, have stood the test of time and are found in recipes the world over. Others, such as frankincense and cassia root, are unknown to most consumers and serve as new toys for distillers to play with. In addition to gin and absinthe, a new wave of flavoured craft spirits is on the rise, such as cinnamon whisky and pink-peppercorn vodka.

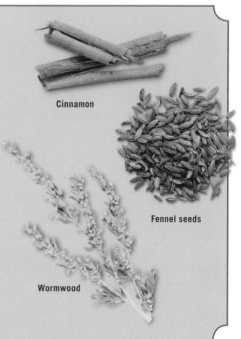

Cinnamon

Fennel seeds

Wormwood

The Stills

The two main types of stills are pot and column varieties. Distillers choose which to use according to preference and the needs of particular spirits.

Spirit and Polish

Many craft producers use different techniques or equipment to enhance quality. Traditionally, producers use small-batch pot stills for flavour-rich spirits, such as brandy, mezcal, and single-malt Scotch, and column stills for neutral spirits, such as vodka and white rum.

Distilling in the Pot Still

Small in size, traditional pot stills are favoured by purists looking to create quality spirits with a nod towards history and authenticity. These dynamic stills – usually made from copper – are labour-intensive, energy-consuming affairs, requiring cleaning and resetting between batches, although modern versions have made technological advancements.

Pot stills make use of simple distillation – a mixture is heated by the boiler, and vaporizes into separate parts, due to the different boiling points of water and alcohol. The vapours condense and are collected as a liquid end product. Single distillation results in a strong, crude spirit, so spirits are usually distilled more than once.

5 Vapour with the lowest boiling point and the highest alcohol content reaches the top

4 Condensing plates span the column; distillers manipulate these to achieve desired flavours

3 The alcohol and water vapours rise up into the column; most condense and fall into the pot

1 The fermented base (a low-proof alcohol known as the "wash") is added to the pot by a tube

2 A heating element pumps steam into a jacket surrounding the pot and brings the wash to its two boiling points

6 A controlled amount of vapour enters this pipe, called the lyne arm

Distillation column

Pot

8 The alcohol drips into a collection vessel, and is often re-distilled, then filtered, and perhaps blended or aged

Distilling in the Column Still

Modern column stills are generally thought to be more efficient and economical than pot stills because they require one distillation as part of a continuous process. Multiple chambers allow for exact separations within a complex liquid, known as fractional distillation. This gives distillers great flexibility, although critics claim that the output can lack character and complexity. Column stills also produce a higher concentration of alcohol in the final distillate, compared to pot stills, which produce low-strength batches.

Some producers use steam distillation in a column still – this involves passing steam through ingredients to distil alcohol or extract essential oils from plant materials.

4 The mixture of alcohol vapours and steam rises to the top of the column

9 At the required strength, vapour condenses at the top and runs through a water-cooled condenser

1 The wash goes through the analyzer column into the rectifier column, where it goes through tubes and ends up inside the analyzer

10 The liquid is collected, and often re-distilled, then filtered, and perhaps blended or aged

7 Vapour flows into a central pipe in this condenser, which is surrounded by a pipe of cold water. As it cools, vapour condenses into liquid ethanol

7 The wash vaporizes, forcing the alcohol up the still, through long curved pipes

3 The wash boils, and vapours rise through a series of plates inside the analyzer column. Depending on their temperature and density, some vapours may become trapped in the plates

2 Steam is fed into the base of the analyzer, and meets the wash on the column's perforated plates

6 The hot vapours enter the rectifier at the bottom, where they meet the wash

Analyzer column

Rectifier column

8 Any solids in the wash fall to the bottom and are recycled or discarded

5 The spent wash runs down and exits from the base

Even the most exquisite drink just isn't a cocktail if you don't serve it with panache. Pay your respects to the art of the cocktail by serving your drink in the correct glass, with complementary and elegant extras.

All About the Glass

Glassware has evolved in order to complement every kind of cocktail. Some vessels are meant to fit certain volumes of liquid, others help to control temperature or release aromas. A speciality shop can sell dozens of shapes and sizes, but for the home consumer, only a handful of styles is really necessary, and it is easy to get creative with what you already have – for example, try using a clean jam jar as a quirky collins glass replacement.

Martini (aka Cocktail)

Cocktails Martini, Manhattan, Cosmopolitan, Blood and Sand

The sloping sides display a stick of olives nicely and prevent the ingredients from separating

Perhaps the most iconic glass design, the Martini glass exudes elegance. Perfect for shaken or stirred drinks without ice (served "up"), the stem prevents your hands from warming the drink, and the conical shape opens up the liquid, thereby enhancing the drink's aromas.

A long stem keeps warm hands away from the cold drink in the bowl

Double Old Fashioned (aka Rocks)

Cocktails Negroni, Sazerac, White Russian, Old Fashioned, Mai Tai, Caipirinha

This is the opposite of the snifter, as the thick base is designed for holding ice, though it can also be used for a neat pour. These are ideal for gin on the rocks, or drinks that require muddling.

The wide mouth is perfect for grated garnishes

Thick base is ideal for holding ice and makes it easier to muddle ingredients

The Crafty Garnish

Bartenders often let their creative juices flow by garnishing with the likes of pickled, crystallized, and dehydrated fruits and vegetables.

Flamed Citrus Peel

For a smoky citrus aroma, prepare a 2.5–5cm (1–2in) round of peel. With care, hold a lit match 7.5cm (3in) above the cocktail. Hold the peel coloured-side down, another 7.5cm (3in) above the lit match. Twist and squeeze the peel over the lit match, then rub the peel around the rim of the glass.

Smoky Ice Cubes

Liquid smoke is an inexpensive, easy-to-use product with a smoky flavour. When making ice cubes, add a few drops to each cube; as the cubes melt into your drink, they impart a smoky flavour that complements strong, bold cocktails, such as a Manhattan or an Old Fashioned.

How to Rim Your Glass

Adding a sweet, salty, or spicy coating to the rim of a glass transforms a cocktail's appearance, mouthfeel, and flavour profile.

1 Rub the rim of a glass with a citrus wedge, or dip the vessel in simple syrup, agave syrup, or the main spirit from your cocktail.

2 Place the glass face-down on a plate covered in your desired coating.

The next level Start with coarse salt or crystallized sugar. You could play around with chilli powder, sweet- or savoury-smoked salt, and ground cinnamon.

Coupe

Cocktails Daiquiri, Sidecar, Gimlet, Corpse Reviver No. 1

Historically used for sipping Champagne, this wide brim is best suited to fragrant cold cocktails

Less top-heavy, and therefore less prone to spilling than the similar Martini glass, the coupe evokes a bygone era when formality reigned in the world of cocktails. The liquid should reach to the top of the glass, ensuring that the drinker's nose stays in close proximity to the aromas.

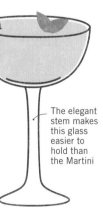

The elegant stem makes this glass easier to hold than the Martini

Collins (aka Highball)

Cocktails Bloody Mary, Mojito, Gin Fizz, Gin Sling, Paloma, Absinthe Frappé

Known in some circles as a chimney-style glass, this tall vessel is used for cold drinks containing a large proportion of non-alcoholic mixers served over lots of ice cubes. Modern bartenders often favour a large jar.

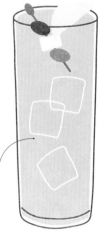

The tall collins glass is perfect for drinks that need to be served super-cold with ice

A Taste for the Good Stuff

Once you've chosen a lovingly made gin, the next step is to try it. Sometimes all you need to enjoy craft spirits is ice or a dash of water. Most producers recommend drinking their spirits at room temperature, but if you prefer, try adding a single ice cube.

HOW TO APPRECIATE

For the best tasting experience possible, have some water on hand to refresh your tastebuds between sips. If you struggle to recognize the characteristics of a spirit, add an ice cube or a dash of water to open it up, but keep in mind that cooling a spirit may dull the aroma and flavour.

When tasting multiple spirits, nibble a plain cracker between tastings to reset your palate. If you are tasting multiple expressions of the same spirit, start with the youngest and lightest, then move on to stronger, darker varieties. Leave a little in each glass so you can go back and forth to discern the differences.

1 The pour Pour a small amount into the glass of your choice. Resist temptation and "drink with your eyes" first – examine the liquid, hold it up to the light, note the colours (which often correlate to flavours), and gently swirl it around the glass to release the aromas. Most spirits don't need to breathe: a spirit that sits too long may experience evaporation and lose character.

2 The nose With your nose about 5cm (2in) above the glass, inhale slowly. Gently swirl and, as your senses adjust, inhale again closer to the liquid. Your olfactory sensors will respond to certain components and affect the way you taste the spirit.

3 The sip Start with a small sip, and let the liquid roll around your tongue. Note the feeling on your tongue and in your throat and nose. Take another sip. Savour it and reflect on whether it suits your palate. If it is abrasive, add an ice cube or a dash of water or soda.

Flavour Wheel

There are thousands of characteristics to look for in spirits, so tasting can seem overwhelming. Use this flavour wheel to help pinpoint your observations. The blue "vegetal" section is particularly useful for tasting gin.

Rums are made from natural sugar cane and molasses so fall squarely into the sweet section of the wheel.

Fruit-based spirits such as brandies and Cognacs are likely to fall into the fruit section of the wheel.

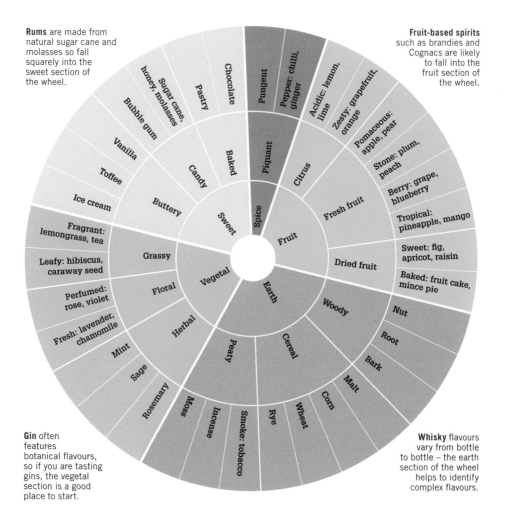

Gin often features botanical flavours, so if you are tasting gins, the vegetal section is a good place to start.

Whisky flavours vary from bottle to bottle – the earth section of the wheel helps to identify complex flavours.

Gin is **growing and growing** in popularity. Independent distilleries, **unique brands**, and trendy cocktail venues are popping up all the time. Learn about the **global suppliers of gin**, with information on reputation, ethos, philosophy, and ingredients. Most importantly, embark on a gin-tastic **tasting journey** in search of your **all-time favourite tipple!**

Gin:
The A-Z

Adnams Copper House

Gin, 40% ABV

DISTILLERY Copper House Distillery, Suffolk, England. Founded in 2010.
PHILOSOPHY An innovative English producer that brews and distils on the same site.

The spirit To create a London Dry gin, Adnams adds six botanicals directly to the base spirit (Adnams barley vodka, made from locally grown East Anglian malted cereals) in a copper pot still.

The taste Elegant and approachable, Adnams' warming flagship gin features a classic juniper punch, followed by floral and citrus notes.

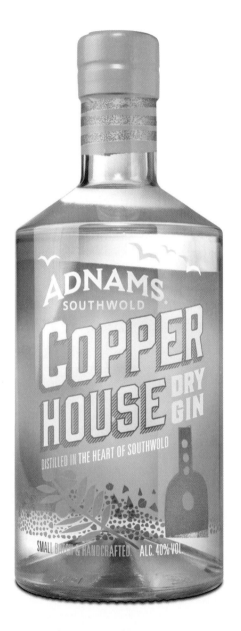

Amato

Gin, 43.7% ABV

DISTILLERY Amato Gin Distillery, Wiesbaden, Germany. Founded in 2014.

PHILOSOPHY Creating a hand-crafted, small-batch, regional gin inspired by Italian flavours.

The spirit Tomatoes and a mix of hand-selected botanicals macerate for roughly 24 hours and then undergo a double distillation.

The taste Fresh scents of citrus, coriander, and peach give way to intriguing flavour notes of thyme, coriander, tomato, and cucumber.

Aviation

Gin, 42% ABV

DISTILLERY House Spirits Distillery, Oregon, USA. Founded in 2004.

PHILOSOPHY One of the Pacific Northwest's most lauded distilleries produces an award-winning spirit inspired by the great American cocktail gins of the pre-Prohibition era.

The spirit Fresh botanicals steep in high-quality American neutral grain spirit for nearly 24 hours to extract flavours. The liquid is then distilled in a custom pot still, and is blended with purified water to reach the desired proof.

The taste This complex gin gets its prized flavour from a balance of traditional and contemporary ingredients, such as cardamom, coriander, aniseed, dried sweet orange peel, lavender, Indian sarsaparilla, and juniper.

The Botanist

Gin, 46% ABV

DISTILLERY Bruichladdich Distillery, Isle of Islay, Scotland. Spirit launched in 2010.
PHILOSOPHY Self-described "progressive Hebridean distillers" use hand-foraged local island botanicals to create an innovative dry gin.

The spirit More than 30 ingredients undergo a slow distillation (to maximize flavour) in an elderly and unique Lomond still that is affectionately known as "Ugly Betty".

The taste With aromas that range from menthol to coriander, this smooth spirit delivers complex and spicy flavours: thyme, coriander, tomato, and cucumber.

Buss No. 509 Raspberry

Gin, 37.5% ABV

DISTILLERY Zuidam Distillers BV, Baarle-Nassau, The Netherlands. Spirit launched in 2014.

PHILOSOPHY With a somewhat unconventional approach, Buss Spirits creates artisanal flavoured gins of fantastic quality.

The spirit The first product from Buss Spirits, this raspberry gin gets its distinctive flavour and colour from fresh raspberries, which are macerated for up to three weeks.

The taste This soft, gentle gin offers a naturally sweet raspberry flavour. It is the perfect "gateway" gin for those who aren't usually fans of the spirit.

Caorunn

Gin, 41.8% ABV

DISTILLERY Balmenach Distillery, Cromdale, Scotland. Spirit launched in 2009.

PHILOSOPHY Artisanal and small batch, this gin is named after the Gaelic word for "rowan berry", a Celtic botanical that forms the backbone of the spirit.

The spirit Master Distiller Simon Buley quadruple-distils this gin in the world's only Copper Berry Chamber. Inside this copper vessel, vapour passes through four trays that are carefully packed with 11 botanicals.

The taste This gin offers a clean and crisp flavour with a long and dry finish.

Citadelle

Gin, 44% ABV

DISTILLERY Logis d'Angeac, Ars, France. Spirit launched in 1997.

PHILOSOPHY The president of Maison Ferrand, Alexandre Gabriel, creates fine gin using an eighteenth-century recipe.

The spirit This recipe calls for a complex medley of spices and a pot still. The production team triple-distils French wholegrain wheat, natural spring water, and a blend of distinct botanicals in copper pot stills. For six months of the year, the same stills are used to distil Pierre Ferrand Cognac.

The taste Soft and smooth on the palate, this subtle gin sports a long aftertaste that fully expresses the spirit's aromatic complexities.

The Cutlass (West Winds)

Gin, 50% ABV

DISTILLERY Tailor Made Spirits Company, Margaret River, Australia. Founded in 2011.

PHILOSOPHY This small distillery benefits from the abundance of rainwater in the local area and top-quality natural resources.

The spirit The base spirit for this gin is an Australian wheat grain variety, which undergoes a one-shot distillation in a copper pot still. The team adds a mix of 12 botanicals to each batch to ensure maximum flavour.

The taste This gin has a creamy white-pepper mouthfeel, accompanied by a cornucopia of unusual flavours, such as cinnamon myrtle, lemon myrtle, and Australian bush tomato.

Death's Door

Gin, 47% ABV

DISTILLERY Death's Door Distillery, Wisconsin, USA. Founded in 2007.
PHILOSOPHY This is a community-minded producer that supports the local economy by sourcing sustainable grains and local ingredients.

The spirit The gin's base spirit is a unique mix of three grains – wheat, barley, and corn. This distillate meshes with a simple botanical mix of juniper berries, coriander seed, and fennel through a vapour-extraction process.

The taste Fronted by a bright nose of fresh juniper, the liquid enters the palate with a creamy mouthfeel, then finishes with a cooling anise note that leaves the mouth fresh and clean.

Dorothy Parker

Gin, 44% ABV

DISTILLERY New York Distilling Company, New York, USA. Founded in 2009.
PHILOSOPHY This lauded New York City distillery creates high-quality and original spirits, celebrating the Prohibition-era American cocktail heritage of the region.

The spirit Making this gin is a time-consuming and labour-intensive process. In a 1,000-litre (220-gallon) pot still, the producer distils a neutral-grain spirit, filtered water, and eight ingredients known as the "botanical build".

The taste This light and balanced gin features hints of juniper and citrus with deep floral notes and subtle fruit.

·HOW TO ENJOY· This is the perfect choice for a Martini.

Dutch Courage

Gin, 44.5% ABV

DISTILLERY Zuidam Distillers BV, Baarle-Nassau, The Netherlands. Spirit launched in 2004.

PHILOSOPHY This family-owned and -operated craft distillery makes use of the best ingredients from all over the world.

The spirit A unique method with separate distillations of nine botanicals in copper pot stills – from Italian iris root and Moroccan coriander to Indian liquorice root – produces a fresh, dry, complex, and layered flavour.

The taste The nose is clean with fresh citrus and earthy juniper notes and a beguiling hint of spice and vanilla.

Elephant

Gin, 45% ABV

DISTILLERY Elephant Gin Distillery, Mecklenburg-Vorpommern, Germany. Founded in 2013.
PHILOSOPHY Inspired by the botanical discoveries of nineteenth-century African explorers, these gin pioneers donate a portion of their proceeds to African elephant conservation efforts.

The spirit A mix of 14 hand-selected botanicals – including fresh apples from the surrounding orchard and rare African ingredients such as buchu, African wormwood, and baobab – are left to macerate in a copper pot still. The staff dilutes the results with local spring water, and distils with neutral spirit.

The taste This smooth spirit stimulates the palate with a mixture of herbaceous, fruity, and spicy notes – unusual to many palates, due to the use of rare African ingredients.

Ferdinand's Saar

Gin, 44% ABV

DISTILLERY AV Distillery, Wincheringen, Germany. Spirit launched in 2013.

PHILOSOPHY This small distillery, nestled near the vineyards that border Germany, Luxembourg, and France, makes an inviting spirit that reflects the flavours of the region.

The spirit Carefully hand-picked Riesling grapes and more than 30 botanicals contribute to this gin's complex flavour.

The taste Locally harvested ingredients, such as quince, lavender, rosehip, angelica, hop blossom, and lemon-scented thyme, complement the acidity from the grapes.

Few Barrel

Gin, 46.5% ABV

DISTILLERY Few Spirits, Illinois, USA. Founded in 2011.

PHILOSOPHY This is a true "grain-to-glass" distillery — the producer ferments local grain, then distils, ages, and bottles everything in-house.

The spirit This gin starts with a high-proof neutral-flavoured alcohol base, distilled from grain. The team infuses this with botanicals and then re-distils it in a dedicated gin still. For six to nine months, it ages in new American oak barrels and used bourbon and rye whiskey barrels.

The taste The mix of oak-like vanilla sweetness and spicy botanical flavour balances the spirit somewhere between a whisky and gin. Notes of cinnamon, grapefruit, vanilla, and black pepper shine through.

Filliers 28°

Jenever, 43.7% ABV

DISTILLERY Filliers Distillery, Bachte-Maria-Leerne, Belgium. Spirit launched in 1928.

PHILOSOPHY This producer distils its own malt wine in traditional copper stills – a carefully guarded family secret recipe, passed down through four generations.

The spirit Distilling jenever is a very delicate balancing act. An experienced Master Distiller observes everything from the grinding of raw materials in the milling unit to the ageing of the juniper distillates in oak barrels.

The taste The pale yellow liquid carries a mild and soft flavour of grains with notes of wood, vanilla, and malt wine.

Fords

Gin, 45% ABV

DISTILLERY Thames Distillers, London, England. Spirit launched in 2012.

PHILOSOPHY Celebrating the great gin heritage of the Master Distiller, Charles Maxwell – an eighth-generation distiller.

The spirit The producer steeps nine botanicals – ranging from Chinese jasmine and Turkish grapefruit peel to Polish angelica – in neutral grain alcohol made from English wheat. Distillation takes place in a duo of unique steel pot stills made by the legendary still-maker, John Dory.

The taste Aromatic, fresh, and floral, this gin yields elegant notes of orange blossom, citrus, and juniper, with a long and smooth finish.

Four Pillars Rare Dry Gin

Gin, 41.8% ABV

DISTILLERY Four Pillars Distillery, Yarra Valley, Australia. Spirit released in 2013.

PHILOSOPHY The first labour of love from Four Pillars Gin, this gin has been made in a truly modern Australian style, combining Asian spice and Mediterranean citrus.

The spirit A clean base characterised with European and Asian spices, native lemon myrtle and Tasmanian pepperberry, and lifted with the warm aromatics of whole fresh organic oranges.

The taste Classic, clean, aromatic, and spiced with enough unique characters to fascinate the hardest gin fanatics. This gin takes the classic G&T to a bold and modern Australian place.

Geranium

Gin, 40% ABV

DISTILLERY Langley Distillery, West Midlands, England. Spirit launched in 2009.

PHILOSOPHY Celebrating decades of experience at one of Great Britain's oldest and finest gin distilleries.

The spirit This classic London Dry gin is made from ten fresh and dry botanicals, which are infused for 48 hours in 100 per cent pure grain spirit made from the finest English wheat.

The taste This gin starts with a crisp and floral aroma, followed by a light flavour of juniper with sweet notes from cassia, orange, and liquorice.

Gin 27

Gin, 43% ABV

DISTILLERY Appenzeller Distillery, Appenzell, Switzerland. Spirit launched in 2013.

PHILOSOPHY Distillers have collaborated with the experts behind a Swiss bar and restaurant to develop a top-quality gin at one of Switzerland's most iconic distilleries.

The spirit These are the producers behind one of Switzerland's most famous herb liqueurs, Appenzeller Alpenbitter. To make their dry gin, the team applies a mix of botanicals to a state-of-the-art distillation system.

The taste Fresh and well-composed flavour notes run the gamut from coriander and citrus zest to cinnamon, nutmeg, and cardamom.

Gin Mare

Gin, 42.7% ABV

DISTILLERY MG Distillery, Barcelona, Spain. Spirit launched in 2010.

PHILOSOPHY Using the best Mediterranean ingredients – all with completely traceable origins – in a tiny 250-litre (55-gallon) craft still.

The spirit The production team distils the ingredients individually for at least 24 hours. They peel the citrus fruits by hand and macerate them for over a year in special jars. Every batch needs 15kg (33lb) of Arbequina olives – these are blended by hand.

The taste This spirit gives off a spicy nose with herbaceous notes of pine, rosemary, tomato, and black olive. The slightly bitter finish contains traces of thyme, rosemary, and basil.

Greenhook Ginsmiths

Gin, 47% ABV

DISTILLERY Greenhook Ginsmiths Distillery, New York, USA. Founded in 2012.

PHILOSOPHY This is an award-winning, small-batch New York City distillery run by the gin-loving DeAngelo brothers.

The spirit The gin is vacuum-distilled, bringing temperatures right down. This protects delicate botanical aromas from being muted by the high temperatures usually associated with the distillation process.

The taste The clean juniper and citrus nose gives way to an elegant, silky texture that lingers on the tongue and a complex and vivid finish.

G'Vine Floraison

Gin, 40% ABV

PRODUCER EuroWineGate Spirits & Wine, Cognac, France. Founded in 2001.
PHILOSOPHY Creating grape-based gins, this company takes a unique approach to gin.

The spirit Unlike many gins, this variety is crafted from grapes. The team enhances the base spirit with ten botanicals, including the rare vine flower from the company's legendary vineyards.

The taste This is a light, vibrantly floral gin that captures the exhilarating essence of the vineyard and the warmth of summer.

Helsinki

Gin, 47% ABV

DISTILLERY The Helsinki Distilling Company, Helsinki, Finland. Founded in 2013.

PHILOSOPHY The first independent distillery in Helsinki produces an artisanal premium gin.

The spirit The team macerates nine hand-picked botanicals (including Arctic lingonberry) in Finnish neutral grain spirit for 24 hours, and then re-distils the spirit. Some of the most delicate botanicals are added to the vapour-infusion tank for extra aroma.

The taste The smooth, pleasant mouthfeel gives way to distinct bursts of fennel, coriander, orris root, and angelica, with a pinch of rose petals.

THE HELSINKI DISTILLING CO.

PREMIUM CRAFT

HELSINKI DRY GIN

50 cl   47% vol

DISTILLED AND BOTTLED BY
THE HELSINKI DISTILLING COMPANY
HELSINKI — FINLAND

Hernö

Gin, 40.5% ABV

DISTILLERY Hernö Gin Distillery, Ångermanland, Sweden. Founded in 2011.

PHILOSOPHY Sweden's first dedicated gin distillery is, for now, the world's northernmost. Two hand-hammered copper stills, known as Kerstin and Marit, are the soul of the distillery.

The spirit The producer distils an organic wheat spirit base twice in the copper stills. They use eight botanicals: juniper, cassia, lemon peel, vanilla, coriander, lingonberries, black pepper, and meadowsweet. The spirit matures for a month in a juniper-wood cask.

The taste Fresh juniper and woody notes shine through this round and smooth gin, with hints of honey and citrus on the finish.

Junipero

Gin, 49.3% ABV

DISTILLERY Anchor Brewing & Distilling Company, California, USA. Founded in 1993.
PHILOSOPHY These innovators helped to spark the modern craft spirits movement in San Francisco and beyond.

The spirit Made by hand in the classic London Dry gin tradition, this spirit was the first post-Prohibition craft gin to be distilled in the United States. The staff distils more than a dozen botanicals in a small copper pot still. To create the secret recipe, the distillers were inspired by the herbs, spices, and botanicals in Anchor Brewing's very own Christmas Ale.

The taste This flavour-forward gin is light, crisp, and clean and combines a deep spiciness with subtle delicacy.

HOW TO ENJOY
Try it in a simple cocktail, such as a Gimlet.

Langley's No. 8

Gin, 41.7% ABV

DISTILLERY Langley Distillery, West Midlands, England. Spirit launched in 2009.

PHILOSOPHY The largest family-owned independent distillery in the UK, Langley uses only traditional methods.

The spirit English wheat grain spirit, water, and botanicals undergo a single distillation in Connie (a 3,000-litre / 660-gallon pot still named after the Master Distiller's late mother).

The taste This kicks off with notes of juniper and coriander, which are followed by a fresh and grassy finish featuring pine notes and a balancing liquorice sweetness.

HOW TO ENJOY
This is delicious mixed with a top-quality tonic.

Letherbee

Gin, 48% ABV

DISTILLERY Letherbee, Illinois, USA. Founded in 2011.

PHILOSOPHY Bartenders who make serious cocktail-friendly spirits with bartenders in mind.

The spirit In a labour-intensive process, a base spirit is enhanced with a balanced blend of 11 botanicals – from coriander and cardamom to peppery cubeb berries. The gin is non-chill filtered so that robust botanicals can shine through.

The taste With a tangible mouthfeel, the spirit tastes of pepper and spice. A versatile and unique spirit that suits classic and craft cocktails.

LETHERBEE ORIGINAL LABEL

LETHERBEE GIN

GIN FOR WELLNESS

1L (48% Alc. by Vol.)

Loyalist

Gin, 40% ABV

DISTILLERY Sixty-Six Gilead Distillery, Ontario, Canada. Founded in 2010.
PHILOSOPHY On an 80-acre (33-hectare) rural farm, this distillery uses highly detailed traditional techniques and state-of-the-art equipment.

The spirit In London Dry-style with no added sugar, this complex gin is made from locally harvested grains and hops, water sourced from limestone-filtered artesian wells, and a mix of locally sourced botanicals, including hand-picked juniper berries.

The taste Full-bodied and elegant, this gin gives off scents of flowers and lavender, with cucumber and liquorice flavours on the palate.

Martin Miller's

Gin, 40% ABV

DISTILLERY Langley Distillery, West Midlands, England. Spirit launched in 1999.

PHILOSOPHY An innovative producer bringing the philosophy of tea-making to gin production.

The spirit The production team distils the dried peels of citrus fruits separately, away from earthy botanicals like juniper – this yields a more balanced, citrus-forward expression. The use of pure Icelandic spring water produces a soft mouthfeel, due to its purity and low mineral content.

The taste The strong citrus introduction gives way to juniper notes, followed by a lovely clean finish and a soft mouthfeel.

McHenry Classic

Gin, 40% ABV

DISTILLERY McHenry Distillery, Tasmania, Australia. Founded in 2010.
PHILOSOPHY This family-run, environmentally sustainable distillery benefits from having five natural springs on site.

The spirit Lovingly hand-made, McHenry's flagship gin is based on rigorous, old-fashioned, hands-on pot-distillation methods. Traditional botanicals are distilled in a Tasmanian-made 500-litre (110-gallon) pot still.

The taste Elegant and smooth, with a rich liquorice flavour, the spirit gives off notes of all the classics: citrus peel, star anise, coriander, cardamom, orris root, and juniper.

The Melbourne Gin Company Dry Gin

Gin, 42% ABV

DISTILLERY The Melbourne Gin Company, Yarra Valley, Australia. Spirit released in 2013.

PHILOSOPHY From the world's most liveable city comes its very own Melbourne Dry Gin. A classic gin with a twist of local flavor, the Melbourne Dry Gin is hand-crafted, batch-distilled and non-chill filtered.

The spirit The traditional foundations of juniper and coriander, blended with locally grown botanicals and the purity of distilled rain water from Gembrook, this gin is a well-rounded, smooth, and subtly surprising spirit.

The taste A contemporary and inspired blend of traditional coriander, juniper, angelica root and cassia bark, with local botanics of organic citrus, rosemary, macadamia, sandalwood, honey, and lemon myrtle.

Monkey 47

Gin, 47% ABV

DISTILLERY Black Forest Distillers GmbH, Loßburg-Betzweiler, Germany. Founded in 2008.

PHILOSOPHY Inside a historic building that dates back to the mid-1700s, this modern distillery features a custom distillation plant, hand-made by the region's famous coppersmiths.

The spirit The production team macerates 47 hand-picked ingredients in a mixture of pure molasses, alcohol, and soft spring water from the sandstone wells of the Black Forest. The spirit matures in traditional earthenware containers for at least three months, and is unfiltered in order to retain a full range of aromas.

The taste An invitingly sweet and flowery aroma with a hint of peppery spices gives way to crisp citrus notes. Notice the subtle bitter fruit notes of cranberries and lingonberries.

Notaris Jonge Graanjenever

Jenever, 35% ABV

DISTILLERY Herman Jansen Beverages, Schiedam, The Netherlands. Distillery founded in 1777.

PHILOSOPHY One of Holland's most lauded distilleries embraces family values, honesty, and hard work to create this jenever.

The spirit This 100 per cent organic gin is made using grains sourced from the mill just behind the distillery, which are then combined with grain alcohol.

The taste A classic Dutch jenever, this sweet, grain-forward spirit offers notes of bread, yeast, and juniper.

No. 209

Gin, 46% ABV

DISTILLERY No. 209, California, USA. Spirit launched in 2005.

PHILOSOPHY Originally established in 1882 when it was the 209th permitted distillery in the United States, this innovative producer makes use of the best Old World distilling techniques.

The spirit The producer creates the gin using single-shot distillation in a copper alembic pot still. The base spirit is four-times column-distilled using Midwestern corn, and the water comes from snowmelt on the Sierra Nevada Mountains.

The taste No. 209 opens with a beautifully aromatic nose of citrus and floral notes. It features bergamot, coriander, and cassia flavour notes.

Pink Pepper (Audemus)

Gin, 44% ABV

PRODUCER Audemus Spirits, Cognac, France. Founded in 2013.
PHILOSOPHY Based in the heart of Cognac, Audemus draws inspiration from traditional distilling techniques, modern alchemy, and a passion for innovation.

The spirit This unusual gin is produced using reduced-pressure distillation – each aromatic macerates separately in alcohol and is then distilled. The producer combines each extract with French wheat spirit, and the final product is non-chill filtered to retain an intense flavour and aroma.

The taste Fresh, spicy notes of pink pepper, juniper, and cardamom are prominent. Over time, the liquid evolves to produce notes of vanilla and honey.

Portobello Road

Gin, 42% ABV

DISTILLERY Thames Distillers, London, England. Spirit launched in 2011.

PHILOSOPHY This forward-thinking producer is committed to exploring and celebrating the history of gin; the spirit was developed at The Ginstitute, one of London's smallest museums.

The spirit English-grown wheat forms the base spirit. The producer distils this spirit with nine carefully selected botanical ingredients from around the world, including orris from Tuscany, juniper berries, Spanish lemon peels, and Indonesian nutmeg. The gin is bottled by hand.

The taste This versatile gin can work in a variety of cocktails. An initial burst of juniper gives way to a sustained, fresh citrus character, before closing with a warm peppery finish.

Ransom Dry

Gin, 43% ABV

DISTILLERY Ransom Wine Co. & Distillery, Oregon, USA. Spirit launched in 2014.

PHILOSOPHY This versatile and award-winning distillery uses labour-intensive, traditional methods to produce spirits with great aromatic intensity and body.

The spirit This gin is made from a base ferment of malted barley and rye and an infusion of botanicals in corn-based spirit. Distillation occurs in a hand-hammered, direct-fired alembic pot still.

The taste Ethereal aromatics of hops and white flowers provide an inviting introduction, followed by a rich and silky liquid that is punctuated by citrus and exotic spices.

Rogue Society

Gin, 40% ABV

DISTILLERY Southern Grain Distillery, Canterbury, New Zealand. Spirit launched in 2014.

PHILOSOPHY From the bottom of the world comes a gin that benefits from more than three generations of experience.

The spirit In a historic nineteenth-century still, the team distils a clean neutral wheat spirit with glacial waters from the Southern Alps of New Zealand and 12 exotic botanicals sourced from around the world.

The taste Subtle floral hints of lavender and orange blossom give way to earthy tones of cinnamon bark and nutmeg, before vibrant citrus and juniper flavours coat the palate.

Sacred

Gin, 40% ABV

DISTILLERY Sacred Spirits, London, England. Founded in 2009.
PHILOSOPHY Using vacuum distillation to create truly original drinks of exceptional quality.

The spirit A total of 12 botanicals are used to make this gin – each is separately macerated and distilled with an English wheat base spirit to retain individual character and depth. The process allows no air contact, and takes at least four weeks.

The taste Almost creamy on the palate with a lush, juniper-led nose, this gin yields flavours of violet flowers, crushed cardamom pods, and cinnamon.

Sacred Gin is a beautifully balanced spirit. It is the triumph of distiller Ian Hart and the Sacred Microdistillery, located in his north London home. The smallest commercial distillery of its kind, Sacred has turned gin on its head by favouring vacuum distillation instead of traditional pot distillation.

What's the story?

Sacred creates a truly unique gin. To retain the individual character of each organically sourced botanical, Hart macerates each one separately in English wheat spirit. The ingredients, including whole citrus fruits, macerate for a very long time: at least four to six weeks with no air contact.

Next, Hart distils the botanicals separately in glassware vacuum stills. The air is sucked out of the stills with a vacuum pump to reduce the pressure, achieving a far lower temperature than pot distillation can. As a result, each distillate remains lush and fresh when it is blended to make the gin – think of freshly cut oranges compared to high-temperature cooked marmalade.

Above The robin and the nightingale in the logo represent Sacred's location in leafy Highgate, London. The poet Keats (who wrote "Ode to a Nightingale") once lived in the area.

Awarded a **Double Gold Medal** at the San Francisco World Spirits Competition, **2013**

22 MAY 2009: First production run of Sacred Gin

2 DAYS: The time it takes **2 PEOPLE** to prepare **80kg (175lb)** grapefruit for maceration

What's next?

In addition to Sacred's classic gin, there are also two flavoured gins (Pink Grapefruit and Cardamom), vodkas and vermouths, and Rosehip Cup – an English alternative to Campari. Also in the works are sloe gin, whiskies, and new products born from trials with distilling, cask ageing, and finishing.

Who is behind it?

Ian Hart (right) has always had an interest in science and was distilling from the age of 11, when he experimented with the likes of nitrogen oxide and chlorine oxide. He studied Natural Sciences at Cambridge and worked in various fields, from cellular telephones to banking on Wall Street. Once he found himself out of a job in 2008, he set about experimenting with gin: a mere 23 experiments later, Sacred Gin was born. Hart runs the company alongside his wife, **Hilary Whitney** (left) who was new to the drinks industry before co-founding the company.

Above To retain all the flavour and aroma, vapours must pass through a final liquid nitrogen-cooled condenser.

Right There are five bespoke stills at Sacred Microdistillery. They were all designed by Hart and made especially for Sacred by a glassware manufacturer.

Sipsmith

Gin, 41.6% ABV

DISTILLERY The Sipsmith Distillery, London, England. Launched in 2009.
PHILOSOPHY Created to bring the lost art and craft of traditional copper distillation back to London, this distillery was the first of its kind to open in London for nearly 200 years.

The spirit Master Distiller Jared Brown is a world-renowned drink historian who trawled the history books for inspiration. The one-shot distillation process takes place in small batches to draw out all the impurities in the English wheat base.

The taste The quintessential expression of the London Dry style, this smooth, bold, and aromatic gin offers bright floral meadow aromas, followed by a growing citrus sweetness, and a hint of spice and violet on the finish.

Sloane's

Gin, 40% ABV

DISTILLERY Distilleries Group Toorank, Zevenaar, The Netherlands. Spirit launched in 2011.

PHILOSOPHY Using natural and unique ingredients in the distillation process to create balanced and smooth products.

The spirit Each of the nine botanicals are distilled individually, and then rested, before being blended to create an exceptionally smooth gin with an exquisite balance of flavours.

The taste This spirit is rich and full of flavour, with juniper definitely in charge. Citrus notes and a smooth finish complete the experience.

Spirit Works

Gin, 43% ABV

DISTILLERY Spirit Works Distillery, California, USA. Founded in 2012.
PHILOSOPHY Running a "grain-to-glass" distillery, the all-female production team mills, mashes, ferments, and distils organic whole grains on site.

The spirit After processing Red Winter wheat, the team applies a mix of eight Californian botanicals (juniper, coriander, cardamom, angelica root, orris root, hibiscus, and fresh zest from lemons and oranges) to the pot still.

The taste Wheat provides a round, slightly sweet base to this balanced gin. The botanicals contribute subtle spice and soft floral and fruit notes.

HOW TO ENJOY
To savour the subtle notes, add just a splash of tonic.

Ungava

Gin, 43.1% ABV

DISTILLERY Domaine Pinnacle, Quebec, Canada. Spirit launched in 2010.

PHILOSOPHY This family-owned orchard and maple grove on mountain slopes began as a producer of ice cider and liqueurs. All products use natural and local Canadian ingredients.

The spirit Using a copper pot still and traditional techniques, this small-batch gin has a distinctive sunshine yellow colour due to six rare botanicals – hand-picked in the wild during the summer – that are native to the Ungava region in Canada's Arctic tundra.

The taste Smooth, fresh, floral, and spicy, this unique spirit features the intriguing flavours of Nordic juniper, wild rose hips, cloudberry, crowberry, and arctic-blend and labrador teas.

V2C

Gin, 41.5% ABV

DISTILLERY Hoofvaartkerk Anno 1857, Hoofddorp, The Netherlands. Spirit launched in 2014.

PHILOSOPHY Once a hobby project, V2C is now a small but successful venture. The team focuses on quality, craftsmanship, natural resources, and a distinguished palate.

The spirit No additives, extracts, or filtering processes invade the small-batch process. The team sources the finest ingredients, such as juniper, angelica, orange, liquorice, laurel, and St John's Wort, from all over the world.

The taste This dry gin has a sophisticated full body. Every ingredient shines through – most especially coriander, cardamom, lemon, and ginger.

Victoria

Gin, 45% ABV

DISTILLERY Victoria Spirits, British Columbia, Canada. Founded in 2008.

PHILOSOPHY Situated on idyllic Vancouver Island, this distillery makes premium spirits that are ideal for high-end, spirit-forward cocktails.

The spirit Each numbered, hand-made batch of the distillery's flagship gin is produced in a German-made, 200-litre (44-gallon) pot still. The team bottle only the best-quality middle part of each run, known as the "heart".

The taste A smooth full-bodied spirit, this gin balances the characteristic evergreen flavour of juniper with notes of citrus, floral, and spice.

Williams GB

Gin, 40% ABV

DISTILLERY Chase Distillery, Herefordshire, England. Founded in 2008.

PHILOSOPHY This family-owned, single-estate distillery pays detailed attention to every stage of the production process. The producer fills and seals each bottle by hand.

The spirit Made from scratch using potatoes from the family farm, this gin is unlike many others (in which a neutral grain spirit is re-distilled with botanicals). The team use juniper buds and berries to ensure the driest results.

The taste Dry juniper jousts for attention with zesty citrus, followed by the warm and spicy notes of cinnamon, nutmeg, and ginger.

MORE TO TRY

Botanica

Gin, 45% ABV

DISTILLERY Falcon Spirits Distillery, California, USA. Founded in 2012.
PHILOSOPHY Making innovative products using the best ingredients available, both locally and internationally.

This bold and well-rounded spirit is made using an intricate process. Flavour is preserved by separately distilling each botanical, such as citrus fruit. The team macerates, freezes, thaws, and vacuum-filters cucumbers. The gin tastes of bergamot, citrus, and cucumber, with a complex finish.

Jensen's Bermondsey

Gin, 43% ABV

DISTILLERY Bermondsey Distillery, London, England. Spirit launched in 2004.
PHILOSOPHY Taking inspiration from the delicate vintage gins of the twentieth century.

The staff adds British wheat spirit, water, and classic botanicals to a John Dore still. The ingredients macerate for 9–15 hours (depending on the ambient temperature), then distillation begins. This smooth and well-balanced gin offers an inviting mouthfeel, with lightly floral aromas and a distinct lemon note on the palate.

Njord

Gin, 40% ABV

DISTILLERY Spirit of Njord, Mellerup, Denmark. Spirit launched in 2014.
PHILOSOPHY To develop Danish gin: small-batch and high-quality with a distinct flavour.

Using a German copper pot still, these makers ferment and distil over a two-month period using a one-shot method. Each batch is crafted, bottled, and labelled by hand. The smooth, complex, and balanced gin features notes of spruce, angelica, coriander, woodruff, and junipers.

The **most botanical** of all spirits, gin responds well to **infusions**. Note the **flavours** in gin that most appeal to you, and then infuse with those same flavours, or try new **complementary ones**. For best results, follow the instructions on pages 72–75. In this chapter, you will also learn some of the most **classic cocktail recipes**, and tricks on how to **reinvent them** with clever twists!

Infusions & Cocktails...

Infusing Gin

Star Anise

A visually stunning infusion, star anise-flavoured gin is perfect if you're a fan of pastis and liquorice flavours.

What you need 50g (1¾oz) star anise; 750ml (1¼ pints) gin.

Infusing time 2–3 days.

The next level Enhance the flavour by adding 1 tablespoon of whole cardamom pods to the mix.

Blueberry

Sweeten your gin by infusing it with cooked blueberries.

What you need 100g (3½oz) blueberries, cooked over low heat for a few minutes until they release juice; 750ml (1¼ pints) gin.

Infusing time 1–2 weeks.

The next level Play around with fresh mint or citrus to offset the sweetness of the berries. If you can find tart sloe berries, simply apply those to this recipe to make your own sloe gin.

Lemongrass

Use sweet and floral lemongrass to complement any gin's botanical flavours.

What you need 2–3 lemongrass stalks, cut into chunks; 750ml gin.

Infusing time 3–5 days.

The next level Toss in a few sprigs of fresh mint to make the infusion crisp and refreshing.

Lavender

For an extra-floral and aromatic expression, infuse gin with lavender.

What you need 1½ tsp dried culinary lavender; 750ml (1¼ pints) gin.

Infusing time 1–2 days.

The next level Adding the peel of one lemon (pith removed) can temper the floral notes.

Grapefruit

Fresh grapefruit adds a pleasingly tart note to any gin.

What you need 1 medium grapefruit, peeled and cut into chunks; 750ml (1¼ pints) gin.

Infusing time 3–5 days.

The next level Up the citrus notes by adding the peel of one lime (pith removed). A small chunk of fresh lemongrass gives a more complex result.

Rosemary

Fresh rosemary helps to heighten the savoury elements in your gin.

What you need 2–3 sprigs of rosemary; 750ml (1¼ pints) gin.

Infusing time 3–5 days.

The next level Add a small sliced cucumber to produce a gin that works beautifully with tonic.

Infusing Spirits

Infusing spirits with flavour is a very simple way to craft your spirits and gets great results. Use this technique and the creative recipes in this book to enhance a bland or nondescript spirit. You can use this method to infuse gin, but also vodka, whisky, rum, brandy, cognac, agave spirits, absinthe, baijiu, and more.

What you need

- 1-litre (1¾-pint) airtight jar, sterilized
- fine kitchen strainer
- muslin or coffee filter
- 750ml (1¼ pints) base spirit
- your flavouring of choice

1 Gather all your equipment. Thoroughly wash all of your flavouring ingredients. You could also use small jars, making several infusions from the same bottle.

2 Prepare your ingredients. For lemon gin, peel five lemons, and use a knife to remove excess white pith. Place the peel in the base of the jar.

3 Fill the jar with the base spirit, in this case gin. Lightly stir with a wooden spoon to distribute the infusing ingredients. Cover the jar tightly.

➤

4 Shake the jar lightly a few times. Examine it to ensure no impurities, such as pips or pith, are inside. Store in a cool, dry place away from sunlight.

5 Check your infusion daily, shaking lightly to distribute the flavours. After three days, taste it every day until you achieve the desired flavour.

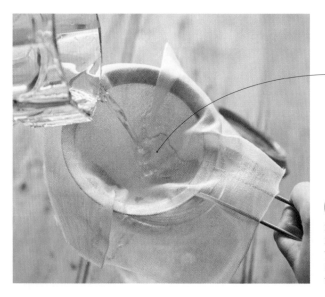

A little sediment is normal, no matter how many times you strain

6 When the infusion is ready, transfer it into a jug then strain into the clean jar using your strainer. Then strain it again using the muslin, and serve.

INGREDIENT KNOW-HOW

Follow the infusing recipes on page 71, maximizing the quality and purity of your infusion with these tips.

- **Air, heat, and large remnants** are your enemy; store your infusion in an airtight container, and strain well.

- **To maximize shelf life**, keep your home-made infusion in the fridge.

- **The base spirit sets the foundation** for your infusion. Start with a less expensive bottle – settle on a good-quality, middle-priced option. The higher the proof, the more flavour you can get from the infusion ingredients.

- **Thanks to its neutrality**, vodka is the most common base spirit. Start with a light spirit; finding the right balance with dark spirits is challenging.

- **Use the freshest ingredients**. Wash all ingredients thoroughly; chop and slice if you like, but discard any elements that you wouldn't eat, such as stems, cores, and leaves.

- **Dried fruit is a breeze** – the flavours are not as bright as fresh fruit, but the finished product's plump, boozy fruit is an additional treat.

TIME IT RIGHT

Refer to these timing guidelines, keeping in mind that the best way to judge when your infusion is ready is by trying it and checking that it suits your palate. After all, you're the one getting gin-spired!

- **Herbs, chilli peppers, vanilla pods, cinnamon sticks:** 1 to 3 days

- **Melons, berries, stone fruits, citrus:** 3 to 5 days

- **Vegetables, ginger, apples, pears:** 5 to 7 days

- **Dried spices:** 7 to 14 days

Martini

The Martini is a grown-up cocktail from the late-nineteenth century that allows gin and vermouth to shine. Everyone agrees on the core ingredients, but an age-old debate persists – is it best shaken or stirred? Experts advocate stirring to prevent bubbles or ice shards. Make a classic, or create your own version – there are now hundreds of "-tinis" to try.

The Classic Recipe

Although the ratio of gin to vermouth varies from bartender to bartender, the classic Martini is always heavy on the spirits, so for best results you must serve it cold.

1 Pour 75ml (2½fl oz) dry gin into a shaker.

2 Add 1 tablespoon dry vermouth, fill with ice cubes, and stir until the mixture is cold.

3 Add 1 dash orange bitters. Stir again and strain into a chilled Martini glass.

Serve it up Garnish with an olive or lemon twist.

Create Your Own Signature Mix

Key Components

1 Pour **75ml (2½fl oz) dry gin** into a shaker.

Aficionados prefer a London-style dry gin (at a high proof), but try a light variety for a smoother taste.

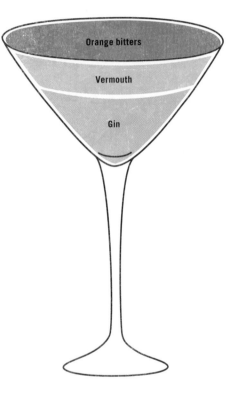

Orange bitters

Vermouth

Gin

2 Add **1 tablespoon dry vermouth**, fill with **ice cubes**, and stir until the mixture is cold.

For a Perfect Martini, swap dry vermouth for equal parts sweet and dry. For a Bone Dry Martini, omit the vermouth, or replace it with a vermouth-rinse or -soaked toothpick to create a Desert Martini.

3 Add **1 dash orange bitters**. Stir again and strain into a chilled Martini glass.

Some recipes omit bitters completely, but they add to the flavour profile. Customize your Martini with a cutting-edge flavour, such as olive bitters.

Additional Flourishes

Garnish As well as a lemon twist or olive, you could use a cocktail onion as a garnish (making a Gibson Martini). Make yours a Dirty Martini by adding a few extra olives and a splash of olive brine.

Skewers Make tomato, olive, and mozzarella skewers, or wrap thin slices of cucumber into a "rose" and secure with a skewer.

➤

CRAFT · REINVENTIONS

Try a change from the classic recipe

The only rule in the Martini game is that there are no rules. Purists scoff, but bartenders take great liberties with the drink – and the **possibilities are endless**.

Spicy Heirloom Tomato Martini

Mix the gin, tomato juice, pickle juice, and horseradish in a shaker. Fill with ice cubes, stir until cold, and strain into a chilled Martini glass. Garnish with the chive blossoms. Serve.

- 3 chive blossoms
- dash of freshly grated horseradish
- 1½ tsp pickle juice
- 30ml (1fl oz) heirloom tomato juice
- 90ml (3fl oz) gin

- chocolate-covered coffee beans
- 30ml (1fl oz) coffee liqueur
- 30ml (1fl oz) cold espresso
- 60ml (2fl oz) vodka

Espresso Martini

Mix the vodka, espresso, and liqueur in a shaker. Fill with ice cubes, stir until cold, and strain into a chilled Martini glass. Top with the coffee beans, and serve.

◀ Cucumber Saketini

Mix the vodka, sake, and cucumber juice in a shaker. Fill with crushed ice, shake for 15 seconds, and strain into a chilled Martini glass. Thread a thin cucumber slice on a skewer, and serve.

- Japanese cucumber slice
- 1 tbsp cucumber juice
- 75ml (2½fl oz) dry sake
- 30ml (1fl oz) vodka

French 75

The French 75 is the world's favourite Champagne cocktail. It can be traced back to 1915, at the New York Bar in Paris – later known as Harry's New York. Bar staff compared the cocktail's kick to that of the powerful French 75mm howitzer gun, and the French 75 was born. Perfect your own version of this simple and elegant cocktail.

The Classic Recipe

The French 75 brings out the best in simple and straightforward flavours and the finest ingredients.

1 Pour 30ml (1oz) dry gin into a shaker.

2 Add 1 tablespoon lemon juice.

3 Add 1 tablespoon simple syrup. Fill the shaker with ice cubes and shake vigorously for 10 seconds.

4 Strain into an iced Champagne flute. Fill to the top with brut Champagne.

Serve it up Garnish with a long lemon twist.

Create Your Own Signature Mix

Key Components

1 Pour **30ml (1oz) gin** into a shaker.
For a stronger drink, double the volume of gin. You could try a complex gin instead of a dry one. If you like sweet flavours, add a dash of brandy or Cointreau.

2 Add **1 tablespoon fresh lemon juice**.
Using fresh lemon juice is always best, but you could also try fresh lime or grapefruit juice.

3 Add **1 tablespoon simple syrup**.
Fill the shaker with **ice cubes** and shake vigorously for 10 seconds.
Simple syrup blends better than sugar alternatives, but mix things up with agave syrup instead.

4 Strain into an iced Champagne flute.
Fill to the top with **brut Champagne**.
There is no need to use high-end Champagne – standard Champagne works very well. For a sweeter option, use rosé Champagne or Prosecco.

Brut Champagne

Simple syrup

Fresh lemon juice

Gin

Additional Flourishes

Garnish Add a touch of jazz with a garnish of candied lemon peel or a slice of root ginger.

Fruit Why not drop a raspberry or blueberry into the glass before you pour? Don't forget to eat it afterwards – it will taste boozy and delicious.

Flowers Add a lightly floral note with some lavender-infused simple syrup, or a dash of pear or elderflower bitters.

➤

These three innovative recipes came from playing around with **fresh fruits and fruity liqueurs** that complement Champagne, and experimenting with **different kinds of bubbles**.

CRAFT · REINVENTIONS

Try a change from the classic recipe

Pear 75

Pour the pear brandy and syrup into a mixing glass. Add ice cubes and stir until cold. Strain into a flute, then top up with Champagne. Garnish with the lemon twist, and serve.

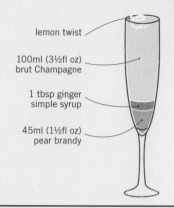

lemon twist

100ml (3½fl oz) brut Champagne

1 tbsp ginger simple syrup

45ml (1½fl oz) pear brandy

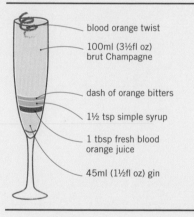

blood orange twist

100ml (3½fl oz) brut Champagne

dash of orange bitters

1½ tsp simple syrup

1 tbsp fresh blood orange juice

45ml (1½fl oz) gin

Blood Orange 75

Pour the gin, juice, syrup, and bitters into a mixing glass. Add ice cubes and stir until cold. Strain into a flute, then top up with Champagne. Garnish with the twist, and serve.

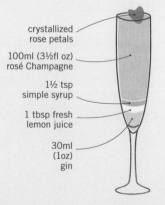

crystallized rose petals

100ml (3½fl oz) rosé Champagne

1½ tsp simple syrup

1 tbsp fresh lemon juice

30ml (1oz) gin

◄ Rosé 75

Pour the gin, juice, and syrup into a mixing glass. Add ice cubes and stir until cold. Strain into a flute, then top up with rosé Champagne. Garnish with crystallized rose petals. Serve.

Gimlet

The Gimlet is the perfect mix of lime juice and gin, and a staple on any classic cocktail menu. You can trace the drink back to the nineteenth century, when sailors mixed it with Rose's lime cordial to make a medicinal tonic. If you're just beginning to mix craft cocktails, start with the Gimlet – it is the perfect platform for many new varieties.

The Classic Recipe

Start off with your favourite gin, grab some fresh lime juice, and you have everything you need for a tart classic Gimlet.

1 Pour 75ml (2½fl oz) gin into a shaker.

2 Add 1 tablespoon fresh lime juice.
Fill the shaker with ice cubes and shake for 10 seconds. Strain into a chilled coupe glass.

Serve it up Garnish with a lime wheel.

Create Your Own Signature Mix

Key Components

1 Pour **75ml (2½fl oz) dry gin** into a shaker.

To best enjoy the tartness of lime, opt for a clean and neutral-tasting gin. For a complex Gimlet, play with flavour-rich craft varieties. Replace gin with vodka for a smooth-tasting Gimlet

2 Add **1 tablespoon fresh lime juice**. Fill the shaker with ice cubes and shake for 10 seconds. Strain into your chilled glass.

Freshly squeezed lime juice lends a tart note; if you seek more sweetness, add simple syrup and reduce the volume of lime.

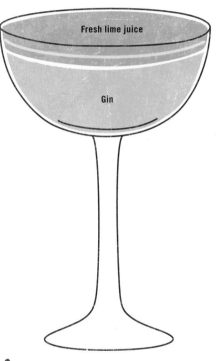

Fresh lime juice

Gin

Additional Flourishes

Garnish A lime wheel is the most common garnish, but you may find a crisp cucumber slice works just as well.

Herbs If you feel like breaking the rules, decorate with a fresh herb (such as thyme or basil) that complements your gin selection.

Berries Tart blueberries and raspberries offer a new flavour dimension – muddle them with lime juice or add them whole.

➤

CRAFT · REINVENTIONS

Try a change from the classic recipe

A Gimlet is not a Gimlet without a tart citrus note, but bartenders often play around with fresh herbs and alternatives to lime. The recipes on the right add a **unique twist**.

Basil Gimlet

Muddle the basil leaves, lime juice, and syrup in a shaker. Add the gin, fill with ice cubes, shake for 10 seconds, and strain into a chilled coupe. Garnish with a basil leaf, and serve.

basil leaf
45ml (1½fl oz) gin
1 tbsp simple syrup
20ml (¾fl oz) fresh lime juice
handful of basil leaves

slice of cucumber
45ml (1½fl oz) gin
1 tbsp simple syrup
5 slices of cucumber
20ml (¾fl oz) fresh lime juice
handful of mint leaves

Cucumber Mint Gimlet

Muddle the mint leaves, lime juice, cucumber, and syrup in a shaker. Add the gin, fill with ice cubes, shake for 10 seconds, and strain into a chilled coupe. Top with cucumber, and serve.

◄ Grapefruit Vodka Gimlet

Combine the vodka, grapefruit juice, and agave syrup in a shaker. Fill with ice cubes, shake for 10 seconds, and pour into a chilled coupe. Garnish with grapefruit peel, and serve.

sliced grapefruit peel
1 tbsp agave syrup
20ml (¾fl oz) fresh grapefruit juice
60ml (2fl oz) vodka

Gin Fizz

The Gin Fizz is the best-known member of the "Fizz" family of cocktails. It was first listed in the cocktail guides of the late nineteenth century. The drink became one of America's most popular choices, forcing bars to employ teams of bartenders to take turns using their muscle to create frothy perfection. Find out how to shake your way to a perfect "Fizz".

The Classic Recipe

This classic gets its trademark froth with an extra-firm shake.

1 Pour 60ml (2fl oz) dry gin into a shaker.

2 Add 30ml (1fl oz) fresh lemon juice.

3 Add 30ml (1fl oz) simple syrup. Fill with ice cubes and shake vigorously for 10 seconds.

4 Fill a collins glass with ice cubes. Strain the mixture from the shaker into the glass.

Serve it up Top with soda, stir, and serve.

Create Your Own Signature Mix

Key Components

1 Pour **60ml (2fl oz) dry gin** into a shaker.
The classic uses a dry gin. For a more complex flavour, replace with a botanical variety.

2 Add **30ml (1fl oz) fresh lemon juice**.
For a more enhanced flavour, swap in mellow and sweet Meyer lemon juice instead.

3 Add **30ml (1fl oz) simple syrup**. Fill with ice cubes and shake vigorously.
When making simple syrup, add an additional citrus peel or fresh mint to complement the flavours.

4 Fill a collins glass with **ice cubes**. Strain the mixture from the shaker into the glass.
Replace plain ice with flavoured ice cubes – add lemon juice or chopped coriander to the water before freezing.

5 Top with **soda**, stir, and serve.
You could use more bubbles or shake the cocktail for longer for extra fizz. Try lemon-flavoured soda, or sparkling wine (known as a Diamond Fizz).

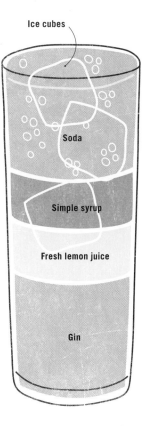

Ice cubes

Soda

Simple syrup

Fresh lemon juice

Gin

Additional Flourishes

Garnish Try ingredients that pair well with gin, such as cucumber, citrus, or fresh herbs.

Froth For a Silver Fizz, add an egg white to the other core ingredients and shake away, or use a whole egg (beaten first, then added to the shaker) to create a Golden Fizz.

Liqueurs Add 1 tablespoon of a liqueur, such as mint or melon, to turn a classic Gin Fizz on its head.

➤

Numerous **Gin Fizz** variations fill cocktail lists all over the world. Fresh eggs are used for extra froth and some mixologists add a **colourful liqueur** to give the drink more impact.

CRAFT · REINVENTIONS

Try a change from the classic recipe

Mint Gin Fizz

Pour the gin, juice, liqueur, and syrup into a shaker. Add ice cubes, shake for 15 seconds, and strain into an ice-filled collins glass. Top up with soda, garnish with lemon and mint, and serve.

slice of lemon and a mint sprig
soda
1 tbsp simple syrup
1 tbsp mint liqueur
1 tbsp fresh lemon juice

60ml (2fl oz) gin

maraschino cherry
2 dashes cherry bitters
soda
1 egg white
1 tbsp simple syrup
1 tbsp fresh lemon juice

60ml (2fl oz) whisky

Whisky Fizz

Mix the whisky, juice, syrup, and egg white in a shaker. Shake for 10 seconds, add ice, and shake again. Strain into an ice-filled collins glass. Top up with soda and bitters, and add the cherry. Serve.

◄ Watermelon Gin Fizz

Pour the gin, juices, and syrup into a shaker. Add ice, shake for 15 seconds, and strain into an ice-filled collins glass. Fill to the top with soda, garnish with watermelon, and serve.

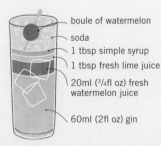

boule of watermelon
soda
1 tbsp simple syrup
1 tbsp fresh lime juice
20ml (³/₄fl oz) fresh watermelon juice
60ml (2fl oz) gin

Gin Sling

The Gin Sling dates to the late eighteenth century. It is often confused with the modern Singapore Sling, but an old-school Gin Sling features fruit brandy and is less sweet than its brilliant-red relative. The sophisticated cocktail is the perfect union of dry, sweet, and sour flavours, and a fantastic choice for new interpretations.

The Classic Recipe

A party favourite, the classic Gin Sling marries dry gin with sweet vermouth.

1 Pour 45ml (1½fl oz) gin into a shaker.

2 Add 30ml (1fl oz) sweet vermouth.

3 Pour in 20ml (¾fl oz) fresh lemon juice.

4 Add 30ml (1fl oz) simple syrup.

5 Add 1 dash Angostura bitters. Shake for 10 seconds.

6 Fill a collins glass with ice cubes. Strain the mixture from the shaker into the glass.

7 Fill to the top with soda.

Serve it up Garnish with a lemon twist.

Create Your Own Signature Mix

Key Components

1 Pour **45ml (1½fl oz) gin** into a shaker.
Opt for a light and clean craft variety.

2 Add **30ml (1fl oz) sweet vermouth**.
Swap in Cointreau, grenadine, or grated nutmeg for sweet vermouth.

3 Pour in **20ml (¾fl oz) fresh lemon juice**.
For a tart flavour, opt for lime juice.

4 Add **30ml (1fl oz) simple syrup**.
Slings need a sweet touch – any mix of simple syrup, caster sugar, grenadine, or pineapple juice works.

5 Add **1 dash Angostura bitters**.
Shake for 10 seconds.
We live in a golden era of bitters – swap in a fun flavour to liven it up.

6 Fill your glass with **ice cubes**. Strain the mixture into the glass.
Use firm, large ice cubes so the drink remains cold.

7 Fill to the top with **soda**.
Soda adds sparkle, but you can replace it with fresh fruit juice.

Ice cubes

Soda

Bitters

Simple syrup

Fresh lemon juice

Sweet Vermouth

Gin

Additional Flourishes

Garnish Impart a bright, clean aroma with a lemon decoration – a twist of peel, wedge, or wheel all work perfectly.

Tartness Add tart fruit, such as sour cherries, to your glass to add oomph to a standard Gin Sling.

CRAFT · REINVENTIONS

Try a change from the classic recipe

Mixologists love to spruce up a standard Sling. Some add fruit liqueurs, and others enhance the tart flavours with different notes of citrus and bitters. These are three of the best variations around.

Aviation

Pour the gin, liqueurs, and juice into a shaker. Add ice cubes, shake for 10 seconds, and strain into a chilled collins glass. Top up with soda. Stir, garnish with the cherry, and serve.

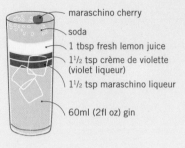

maraschino cherry

soda

1 tbsp fresh lemon juice

1½ tsp crème de violette (violet liqueur)

1½ tsp maraschino liqueur

60ml (2fl oz) gin

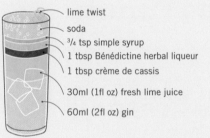

lime twist

soda

¾ tsp simple syrup

1 tbsp Bénédictine herbal liqueur

1 tbsp crème de cassis

30ml (1fl oz) fresh lime juice

60ml (2fl oz) gin

Oahu Gin Sling

Pour the gin, juice, liqueurs, and syrup into a shaker. Add ice, shake for 10 seconds, and strain into an ice-filled collins glass. Top up with soda, and stir. Garnish with the twist, and serve.

◄ Pomegranate Gin Sling

Pour the gin, juice, and syrup into a shaker. Add ice, shake for 10 seconds, and strain into an ice-filled collins glass. Top up with soda, garnish with the pomegranate and lime, and serve.

lime wheel and pomegranate seeds

soda

1½ tsp simple syrup

30ml (1fl oz) fresh pomegranate juice

60ml (2fl oz) gin

Klaus St. Rainer has been working in **bars** and **hotels** for almost 25 years and in 2010 he was given the opportunity to take over the **Golden Bar** in **Munich**, along with his partner **Leonie von Carnap**. During this time, he acquired a formidable amount of experience. Highlights include the five years he spent as a bar manager with **Ernst Lechthaler** in his international bar-catering outlets from **Los Angeles** to **Dubai**, as well as the subsequent seven years he spent fine-tuning his skills in **Schumann's bar** in **Munich** ...

Become a mixology maestro...

Shake up something spectacular
under the expert eye of KLAUS ST. RAINER

Masterful Mixology

FROM BEHIND the world's bar counters I have witnessed not only the bleakest of times for the cocktail, but also the dawn of a new **GOLDEN COCKTAIL ERA** at the end of the 1990s. This has had a formative impact on my own style, as have my travels to source the products I work with and my countless books. From the sugar fields of **MEXICO**, to **SCOTLAND**'s single malt distilleries and the coffee roasters in **AUSTRALIA**, I travel the world in search of **NEW EXPERIENCES** and **ideas**.

Now I'm putting this knowledge into practice at the Golden Bar. **The Golden Bar** was opened in 1937 in the Haus der Kunst (House of Art) in Munich. After the war, the **gilded interiors** with their **global drinks-themed facades** disappeared behind whitewashed walls. These rooms, steeped in history, were "**rediscovered**" in 2003, and creatively and conscientiously re-interpreted, introducing **new ideas** – and that is exactly how I deal with the drinks in this chapter. Most are based on **classics**, which I transform with the help of **modern concepts** and **technology**.

My philosophy throughout is quite simple: never accept anything but **the best.** I have always resisted working with products that don't live up to my idea of quality. **A drink is the sum of its ingredients** – which is something always to keep in mind. All the drinks you see in the photos were produced with the **listed ingredients** and photographed in the Golden Bar. Furthermore, the glasses and utensils used are sometimes **originals** that are up to **200 years old**.

Finally, amid all this **creativity** I have never forgotten the importance of **excellent customer service**, which as bartenders we must provide day in and day out. Only once you have gained your customer's **complete trust** can you fulfil your mission as a **true cocktail evangelist**.

Golden Bramble

It doesn't take much to give simple drinks a certain little something extra. Here a small injection of high-quality orange liquer gives a great "Aha!" effect.

Ingredients

- 50ml (1¾fl oz) gin
- 30ml (1fl oz) fresh lemon juice
- 2 bsp icing sugar
- 20ml (¾fl oz) orange liqueur such as Bigallet China China or Amer Picon

Special equipment

- small cannula
- cocktail glass

Preparation

Vigorously shake the gin, juice, and sugar in a shaker with solid ice and strain into a glass filled with crushed ice. Top up with some more crushed ice. Put the orange liqueur into the cannula and stick the cannula into the drink. Inject the orange liqueur into the drink just before drinking.

Yamahai

Gin and sake complement each other perfectly. In this twist on an improved gin cocktail the fruity notes of gin combine beautifully with the gentle floral notes of the first rate Daiginjo sake.

Ingredients

- 1 unrefined sugar cube
- 30ml (1fl oz) gin
- 30ml (1fl oz) Junmai Daiginjo sake
- 2 dashes orange bitters
- 1 piece lemon zest for squeezing

Preparation

Place all the ingredients in the glass. Crush the sugar cube with the end of a spoon and stir until it dissolves. Then add ice cubes and stir until sufficient meltwater has been produced so that the glass is full to about a finger width below the rim. Squeeze a little bit of lemon zest over the drink (see picture, right).

Ichigo Ichie

In Japan, Ichigo Ichie stands for a chance meeting, the perfect first impression – as perfect as the union of Junmai sake with gin and vermouth.

Ingredients

- 20ml (¾fl oz) Tanqueray No. TEN gin
- 40ml (1¼fl oz) Junmai Sake
- 40ml (1¼fl oz) Carpano Antica Formula Vermouth
- Orange and lemon zest for squeezing

Preparation

Stir all the ingredients in the beaker with lots of ice, and squeeze over a little bit of orange and lemon zest (see picture, left).

Gintelligence No. 1

The template for this hot drink is the classic Tom Collins, which is often confused with the Fizz. In composition these two are almost identical; however, the Fizz is served in a pre-chilled glass without ice and mixed with a shot of soda, while the Collins is served in a long drink glass and diluted with lots of soda. Gintelligence No. 1 got its name because I discovered quite accidentally how fantastic this renowned concoction tasted warm: a crafty drink to warm you up on cold days in autumn and winter. It has an even fuller, stronger flavour if you use Dutch style gin (Jenever) instead.

Ingredients

- 60ml (2fl oz) Dutch style gin
- 30ml (1fl oz) fresh lemon juice
- 20ml (¾fl oz) triple syrup (p.123)
- 5 juniper berries
- 100ml (3½fl oz) hot water

Preparation

Heat all the ingredients except for the water in a saucepan or silver pot on the stove and top up with hot water. Place the juniper berries in a tea cup and serve the drink in the cup or in a soup bowl.

Pink Gin

In its day pink gin was drunk aboard British navy ships. Alcohol was used medicinally to combat infectious diseases and so gin was a fundamental component in any ship's galley. Since it usually had a higher percentage alcohol content than today it would have been diluted 1:1 with cold water. Peak flavour and aromas for a spirit are usually experienced at around 25 per cent alcohol content. I recommend this drink not for medicinal purposes, but because it provides a pleasurable opportunity to try new varieties of gin. More variations can be produced if you try out various bitters; their spicy notes help round off the flavour.

Ingredients

- 50ml (1¾fl oz) ice cold gin
- 50ml (1¾fl oz) ice cold still water
- 5 dashes Sexy Bitters or other bitters

Preparation

Chill the gin in the freezer at −18°C (−4°F). Rinse out a wine glass with a couple of ice cubes. Tip the melt water away and add 5 dashes of bitters to the glass. Tilt and turn until the glass is thoroughly moistened on the inside. At this stage, I recommend smelling deep down inside the glass. Pour in the ice-cold gin, swill round again, and smell once more. Add the iced water, swill briefly, and enjoy.

Dry Martini

One of the earliest mentions of the Martini cocktail is found in Thomas Stuart's book *Stuart's Fancy Drinks and How to Mix Them* from 1896: a well-balanced beverage consisting of one-third dry French vermouth, two-thirds dry gin, bitters, and the zest of a lemon. Unfortunately over the last century the Dry Martini has degenerated into a simple glass of schnapps. Ernest Hemingway is partially responsible for this as he gave the green light for the evolution of increasingly dry martinis with his 15:1 variant. The situation was truly brought to a head by Ian Fleming when he allowed 007 to consume vodka instead of gin in this wonderfully aromatic classic.

Ingredients

- 60ml (2fl oz) gin
- 30ml (1fl oz) dry vermouth
- 2 dashes orange bitters
- 1 small piece lemon zest for squeezing

Preparation

Fill a mixing glass with ice and stir without any other ingredients. Pour off the melted water. Add gin, vermouth, and bitters and stir to chill. Strain into a pre-chilled cocktail glass and scent with the lemon zest so that the essential oils from the peel float over the surface of the drink.

Golden Bartini on the Rocks

Every bar needs its "signature Martini cocktail". Our twist is based on one of the earliest mentions of the dry Martini in Thomas Stuart's mixing book from 1896; I just use Lillet Blanc instead of dry French vermouth. In the Golden Bar this is served on real "rocks", namely deep frozen pebbles from the river Isar. It doesn't matter what pebbles you choose as long as they are smooth. These keep the drink nice and cool without diluting it: because the composition is perfect just as it is straight from the mixing glass.

Ingredients

- 60ml (2fl oz) gin
- 30ml (1fl oz) Lillet Blanc
- 2 dashes orange bitters
- 1 small piece lemon zest for squeezing
- frozen smooth pebbles

Preparation

Stir all the ingredients 72 times in a mixing glass with double frozen ice cubes and pour into an Old Fashioned glass with the frozen pebbles. Add the scent of a little piece of lemon zest, but don't put the whole zest into the drink.

Haus der Kunst Cocktail

This is my own creation, which I have dedicated to the Haus der Kunst ("House of Art") museum in Munich where the Golden Bar is located. The modern artistic transformation of the bar with works by Florian Süssmayr offers a stimulating contrast to the very classical museum space. That's how the drink should be, too. It is based on the French 75, a champagne cocktail with gin, sugar, and lemon, which is first mentioned by Harry Craddock in 1930 in *The Savoy Cocktail Book*. It is served on large ice cubes in an Old Fashioned glass and topped with a gin and tonic foam.

Ingredients

- 50ml (1¾fl oz) gin
- 30ml (1fl oz) fresh lemon juice
- 2 bsp (p.126) icing sugar
- Perrier Jouët Grand Brut champagne
- Gin and tonic foam (p.124)
- Campari dust (p.124)

Preparation

Vigorously shake together the gin, lemon juice, and sugar with solid ice and strain into an Old Fashioned glass filled with ice cubes. Top up with a bit of champagne and spray on the gin and tonic foam to crown it off. Decorate with a pinch of Campari dust.

London Buck

In the Golden Bar, we serve ginger beer hot or cold and without any extras all day long: just a generous squeeze of orange into the glass or cup and enjoy. When enjoyed cold this is a deliciously refreshing beverage, and when heated it is a tasty, warming medicinal substance that you can drink cup after cup of without a care, even if you haven't got a cold.

Ingredients

- 50ml (1¾fl oz) gin
- 120ml (4fl oz) ginger beer, preferably homemade
- squeeze of fresh lime

Preparation

Build up all the ingredients on ice in the glass.

Royal Hibiscus Gin Fizz

The fizz family is clearly defined. A fizz consists of a spirit, something sweet, and something sour, all spritzed up with a touch of soda. If the fizz gets an additional "silver" in its name, the bartender knows that the recipe should have an egg white added. A golden fizz gets an egg yolk and a royal fizz an entire egg. This gives the drink a silky texture and the egg white also ensures a beautiful foamy crown. If the sugar is replaced by liqueur the whole thing is known as a Fix. The Royal Hibiscus Gin Fizz is an unbelievably alluring combination, which is characterized by the dry fruity notes of the hibiscus cold drip and, just for once, is served on ice in a long drink glass.

Ingredients

- 50ml (1¾fl oz) hibiscus cold drip (p.125)
- 1 tbsp fresh lemon juice
- 1 tbsp fresh lime juice
- 2 bsp icing sugar
- 1 egg
- soda for topping up
- dried hibiscus flowers for decoration

Preparation

Vigorously shake all the ingredients except the soda with solid ice in a shaker for at least 15 seconds and strain into a glass filled with ice cubes. Top up with some soda and garnish with pretty hibiscus flowers.

Gintelligence No. 2

This warming and powerful beverage is "gintelligent" and almost more of a medicine than a cocktail. Chamomile calms and relaxes the muscles, while the elderflower cleanses and stimulates the body. It is especially good in winter when you come in from the chilly outdoors or if you're starting to come down with a cold: a perfect "good night cap".

Ingredients

- 200ml (7fl oz) bottle extra dry tonic water, such as Golden Monaco
- 50ml (1¾fl oz) gin
- 2 tsp elderflower syrup
- 1 chamomile tea bag

Special equipment

- silver pot and little cup or silver goblet

Preparation

Pre-warm a tea pot and cup by filling them with hot water. Heat the tonic water in a pan or with the steam nozzle of an espresso machine to just below boiling. Empty the water from the pot. Add the gin and syrup, hang the tea bag inside, and pour over the tonic water. Put the lid on and leave to steep for a few minutes. Serve in a little tea cup or silver goblet.

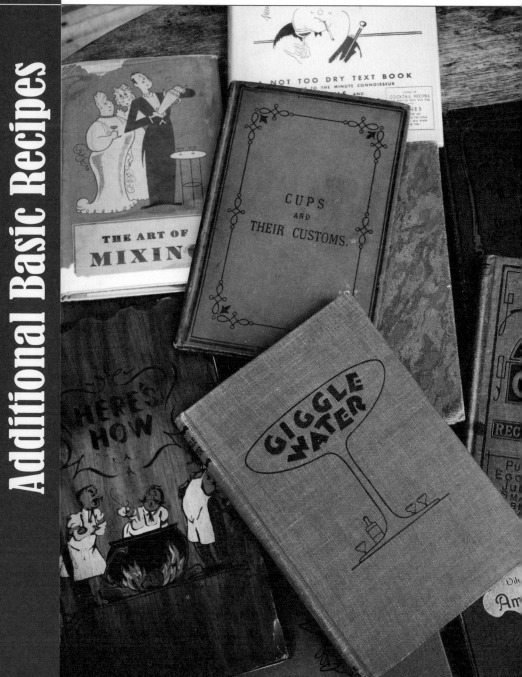

On these pages you will find instructions for some useful home-made ingredients. The syrup recipes can be made on the stove in a small saucepan, but it's also worth trying out the techniques below, as these will enable you to achieve even better results from a taste point of view.

Sous vide

No longer a kitchen novelty, sous vide produces great results when making syrup. Ingredients retain their flavour by cooking them in a vacuum pouch and at a low temperature. What's more, this technique prevents fruit syrups from going cloudy. If you don't own a sous vide device, you can cook heat-resistant vacuum pouches at 60°C (140°F) in your dishwasher.

Quick infusion under pressure

With the "quick method" the sugar syrup is put into a device known as a whipping syphon along with the herbs or spices, and then 2 nitrous oxide cartridges are inserted. The nitrogen dissolves in the liquid and penetrates the cell walls of the ingredients. After just one minute you can carefully release the gas from the syphon, which must be standing upright at this point, whereby the nitrogen bubbles out of the ingredients' cell walls and consequently imbues the liquid with an incredible flavour. Filter and it's ready!

Deep freezing

Syrups made with delicate and aromatic herbs such as basil are best made by filling a vacuum pouch with the relevant herb and adding the sugar syrup to this. Vacuum seal and store overnight in the freezer, then defrost and filter. The results are very delicate, but also wonderfully aromatic.

Sugar syrup

When I refer to sugar syrup (simple syrup) I always mean a ratio of 1:1 white sugar to water, so for example 500g (1lb 2oz) sugar to 500ml (16fl oz) water. If a strong syrup (rich syrup) is required, the ratio is 2:1, and in a light sugar syrup 1:2.

Preparation: bring the water and sugar to the boil until the sugar has completely dissolved. Leave to cool, decant into a clean bottle, and store in the fridge. Sugar syrup can also be produced without heating by simply leaving the mixture at room temperature and occasionally stirring with a balloon whisk. After 30–60 minutes the syrup will be clear. You can significantly extend the shelf life of any syrup by adding a tablespoon of vodka. Normal sugar syrup should keep a good month in the fridge, and with a little shot of vodka it will keep for up to three months; syrup that has been prepared without heating, however, lasts for considerably less time.

➤

Falernum

This is a kind of rum and spice syrup that is essential for many tiki drinks.
Ingredients: 1 cinnamon stick, 8 coffee beans, 4 cardamom pods, 6 allspice berries, 2 pieces star anise, ½ tonka bean (grated), ¼ nutmeg (grated), 2 finely chopped vanilla pods, 1 pinch sea salt (such as fleur de sel), 1 pinch black pepper, 200g (7oz) peeled finely chopped ginger, zest from 2 organic lemons and 2 organic oranges, 600ml (1 pint) Myers's rum, 600ml (1 pint) water, 1kg (2¼lb) sugar.
Preparation: grind all the spices with a pestle and mortar or pulse briefly in a food processor. Toast the spices, citrus zest, and ginger in a pan over a moderate heat then add the sugar and caramelize. Carefully quench with rum and water and leave to simmer for around 10 minutes. Leave to cool, then filter through a fine sieve. Pour into a clean bottle and store cold.

Grenadine syrup

Making grenadine from fresh pomegranates isn't worth the effort. The result has a very short shelf life and its colour produces rather brown drinks. My tip: buy a good brand of pomegranate juice and blend 1:1 with white sugar. Reduce the juice in a microwave on a moderate power setting until it is reduced by half. Stop and stir every so often to completely dissolve the sugar. You will be thrilled! Test and add sugar to taste. The syrup should have a lovely balance between sweetness and acidity.

Raspberry syrup

Gently simmer 750g (1lb 10oz) fresh raspberries with sugar syrup for 20 minutes. Once cool, filter, decant into a clean bottle, and store in the fridge. The sous vide method is recommended here.

Elderflower syrup

Take 100g (3½oz) fresh, clean elderflower heads and bring to the boil with 1 litre (1¾ pints) water, the zest of an organic lime, and 500g (1lb 2oz) sugar. Remove from the hob and stir in 15g (½oz) ascorbic acid to make the syrup last longer. Store in a cool place for 24 hours and then strain through some coffee filter paper. Decant into a clean bottle and store in the fridge.

Chamomile syrup

Bring 500ml (16fl oz) water to the boil with 500g (1lb 2oz) sugar until the sugar has dissolved. Add 3 heaped tablespoons dried chamomile flowers and leave to infuse for 20 minutes without boiling. Strain, decant into a clean bottle, and store in the fridge. Again the sous vide method is recommended here as it results in fewer bitter substances being dissolved. The freezer and quick infusion methods also work well.

Peppermint syrup

To give a julep a bit of a boost, I like to use a little shot of light peppermint syrup. The deep freeze method works best here: simply take a bunch of fresh mint and freeze for 24 hours with 1 litre (1¾ pints) sugar syrup, then thaw and filter.

Lapsang souchong syrup

Boil up 500g (1lb 2oz) sugar with 500ml (16fl oz) water, remove from the hob, and stir in 2 tablespoons lapsang souchong tea. Leave to infuse for 10 minutes, filter into a clean bottle, and store in the fridge. The syrup also produces an exquisite iced tea: make some strong tea and add syrup, ice cubes, a splash of water, and a couple of slices and some juice from an orange and a lemon.

Lime juice cordial

Bring to the boil 1 litre (1¾ pints) sugar syrup with 250ml (9fl oz) freshly squeezed lime juice and the zest of 4 organic limes and leave to infuse for 15 minutes. Cool, strain, and store in a clean bottle in the fridge.

Malt beer syrup

Bring 500ml (16fl oz) non-alcoholic malt beer to the boil with 500g (1lb 2oz) light muscovado sugar, and simmer gently until the liquid has reduced by around a half.

Rock candy syrup

Heat rock candy (rock sugar) and water in a ratio of 1:1 in a saucepan until the sugar has completely dissolved. Pour into a clean bottle and store in the fridge. I particularly like to use this syrup as a sweetener for macerations, for example, in agave coffee (see p.125).

Runny honey

This is the answer if you want to mix drinks with honey – it often lends more depth and texture to a drink than sugar syrup, but it is difficult to dissolve in cold ingredients.
Preparation: stir 2 parts honey together with 1 part hot water until the honey has completely liquefied. It remains liquid even if you put the mixture into a clean bottle and store in the fridge.

Triple syrup

This is similarly a secret weapon for adding a bit more depth and complexity to drinks. Blend equal parts sugar syrup, runny honey, and agave syrup, then decant into a clean bottle. Often a little dash of this is all it takes to round off a drink perfectly.

Gardenia mix

This consists of honey and butter in equal proportions. Heat honey in a pan to liquefy it before adding the butter and whisking the mixture until smooth using a balloon whisk. Pour into a clean jar with a lid and store in the fridge. Allow to soften a little at room temperature before use.

Spice butter

In a food processor, finely grind 1 tablespoon each of cocoa powder, ground coffee, and ground cinnamon with 1 star anise, 3 cloves, and 2 cardamom pods and stir into 100g (3½oz) soft butter. Leave the mixture to infuse for one day in the fridge, allow to soften at room temperature, and press through a fine mesh sieve. Shape the resulting mixture and store in the fridge.

→

Dust

This is a dried ingredient that is ground to a fine powder. By following the recipe here you can make dusts such as Campari dust (see p.112) or Chartreuse dust. Pour 350ml (12fl oz) of the spirit into a plastic baking mould and allow to dry for 1–2 days at 60–70°C (140–158°F) in a dehydrator (see p.128). The liquid and the alcohol will evaporate leaving behind sugar crystals, which taste clearly of the alcohol. Use a pestle and mortar to grind the crystals fairly finely, and store in a dry container in a cool place. You can also make dust in the oven. Leave the oven door open very slightly for a 2–3 day drying period so that the alcohol vapour can escape.

Hibiscus sugar

Place a few dried hibiscus flowers and some fine white sugar in an electric food processor and mix for a couple of seconds. The result is a light pink coloured sugar with dark red reflexes and the wonderfully sharp fruity aroma of the hibiscus.

Espuma

This means foam and it can be made from any liquid you fancy. These foams enhance lots of recipes because they help provide an extra taste dimension. All you need is a cream syphon and 1–2 measuring spoons of xanthan or 1–2 egg whites depending on how firm the foam should be. Xanthan is a plant-based alginate and is used to thicken liquids. If you don't have a syphon you can also beat the liquid with xanthan in a bowl. For foams prepared in a syphon always shake well before use and lather onto the drink. By following the recipe here you can froth up any fruit juice of your choice. The quantity of xanthan might have to be increased slightly.

Creamy orange foam

Pour 500ml (16fl oz) fresh orange juice through a tea strainer so that the pulp doesn't clog up the syphon. Beat the juice with two measuring spoons of xanthan in a food processor for 5 seconds, then pour into the cream syphon, insert 1 nitrous oxide cartridge, and store in the fridge.

Gin and tonic espuma

Place 100ml (3½fl oz) gin, 150ml (5fl oz) tonic water, 50ml (1¾fl oz) lime juice, 30ml (1fl oz) sugar syrup, and 2 egg whites in a cream syphon. Insert 2 nitrous oxide cartridges and leave to rest in the fridge before use.

Bananaruma

Select a container that can be tightly sealed and pour in 1 bottle Anejo rum (700ml/ 1¼ pint), add 50g (1¾oz) dried banana chips and 30g (1oz) desiccated coconut, then leave to macerate at room temperature for 2 days. Open, strain, and decant into a clean bottle.

Sloe gin

Sloe gin is made by flavouring the gin with ripe sloes. The process of flavouring a cold liquid by putting in fruits, herbs, or spices is called maceration. The sloes should either be picked after the first frost or should be frozen initially for 1–2 days in the freezer. This lowers the water content and increases the sweetness in a similar way to grapes used for wine. Commercially produced sloe gin often has added sugar and colourings. By using my method you don't need any sugar – you can always sweeten it later in the drink. The only disadvantage of the natural maceration method is that the sloe gin oxidizes when exposed to light and oxygen, causing its colour to change week by week from a vivid blood red into a brownish red.

Preparation: Fill a clean bottle two-thirds full with sloes that you have either lightly pressed or pricked with a needle and pour in some good-quality gin. Leave in a cool place for 2–3 weeks, and from the second week check and test the gin. When the desired colour and intensity have been achieved, the gin can be filtered through a fine sieve and decanted into a new, impeccably clean, dark bottle. The aroma will be acidic and fruity.

Cold drip

The cold dripper is a Japanese coffee machine for making cold brewed coffee (see p.128), which you can also use to produce highly aromatic alcoholic macerations without bitter substances. This is done by allowing a spirit, for example, gin, to drip through a filter of, for example, chamomile flowers, hibiscus flowers, or nettles. For a 700ml (1¼ pint) bottle, this process takes around 24 hours. On the right is my recipe for nettle cold drip, which also works with other ingredients with some simple modifications.

Nettle cold drip

Fill the filter chamber of a cold dripper with dried stinging nettle leaves. Scald the leaves in the filter chamber briefly with boiling water so that the maceration is a lovely green, rather than a brown, colour. Pour a bottle of gin (700ml/1¼ pints) into the water tank and let it slowly drip through. Then decant into a clean bottle and store in the fridge. The cold drip will keep for several weeks, but will gradually turn darker and browner through oxidization and light exposure.

Beetroot cold drip

Fill the filter chamber with dried beetroot chips and macerate with gin. You will find beetroot chips in a health food shop.

Hibiscus cold drip

Place dried hibiscus flowers in the filter chamber and macerate with gin.

Agave coffee

Place 80g (2¾oz) South American arabica coffee in the filter chamber of the cold dripper. Moisten with Tequila Reposado and pour the rest of the bottle into the water tank. Set the drip rate to 2 seconds per drop. Finally, sweeten with 20–40ml (¾–1¼fl oz) rock candy syrup (see p.123).

Equipment

Using the right equipment for mixing is just as important as having top-notch ingredients. To begin, you don't need much more than a shaker, mixing glass, and a strainer. If you want to delve in a bit deeper, you should consider acquiring a dehydrator or cold dripper.

Shaker

This is used for the preparation of shaken drinks. One variety is the Boston shaker, which consists of a glass section with a metal section that fits over it. Alternatively, you can use two-piece metal shakers and three-piece shakers, which usually have an integral sieve underneath the cover flap that saves you having to use a strainer. The latter, however, are best suited to drinks with clear ingredients. The best options are shakers that are completely metal, or shakers made from precious metals, because drinks created in these will be noticeably colder (see p.129, picture 13).

Mixing glass

This is a large glass with a pouring lip in which all stirred drinks are prepared (see p.129, picture 13).

Strainer

A bar strainer with a spiral is called a Hawthorne strainer. This fits perfectly onto a Boston shaker or a two-piece metal shaker. A one-piece bar strainer without the spiral is called a julep strainer. The julep strainer fits particularly well into most mixing glasses. Both varieties (picture 1) are used to strain ice from a drink.

Tea strainer

A small tea strainer (picture 2) can be held between the strainer and the glass to strain out fine pieces of ice or fruit.

Bar spoon

This is used for stirring drinks, as a bar measure (1 bsp = 5ml), and the flat end can be used to crush small, not too hard ingredients such as sugar cubes (picture 3).

Measuring cup

You can use this to start with to mix up the recipes correctly (picture 4), although you should also train yourself to pour without one. Practise with water, pouring it out and then checking your measure afterwards. Soon you'll be pretty confident, and working without using a measuring beaker looks far more impressive.

Tongs

You can use tongs to move individual ice cubes, sugar cubes, or fruit decorations hygienically and elegantly. My favourites are the large tweezer tongs (picture 5) or metal chopsticks (picture 6).

Equipment

Ice pick and ice scoop

You will need an ice pick to knock large chunks and (with a bit of practice) ice cubes out of a block of ice. For reasons of hygiene, the ice scoop shouldn't be left lying on the ice after use (see p.127, picture 7).

Knife

A sharp knife is needed for lots of bar tasks, from cutting up fruit to carving out shapes from ice. I have a preference for small, Japanese knives, such as the Global brand (see p.127, picture 8).

Muddler

A professional muddler or a 30cm (12in) long wooden pestle is used for mashing or muddling fruits and for crushing ice (see p.127, picture 9).

Atomiser

To imbue glasses with a particular aroma, you simply fill a little scent bottle with the desired ingredient and moisten the glass from the inside using the spray (see p.127, picture 10).

Fine grater

This is used for grating ingredients such as nutmeg or lemon zest (see p.127, picture 11).

Lemon squeezer

Pressing by hand will produce the best juice. For small citrus fruits the so-called elbow press is recommended (see p.127, picture 12). For larger fruit, a free-standing juicer is easier to handle. Even the traditional juicers, where you twist the halved fruit on a ridged cone, give excellent results. For larger quantities of juice, you can also use an electric juicer.

Juicers

An electric juicer (centrifuge) is indispensable for producing juices from ingredients that can't be pressed, such as apple, pineapple, or ginger.

Electric mixer

This is used for creating frozen drinks, for preparing foams (see p.124), or for grinding spices.

Whipping syphon & soda syphon

A whipping syphon is useful, for example, to produce fresh syrup quickly (see p.122). I also use it for sophisticated foams (see p.124). A soda syphon aids the carbonisation (the addition of carbon dioxide) of lemonades and other beverages (picture 15).

Cold drip

A cold dripper is a Japanese coffee machine for making cold brew coffee. In this method, (iced) water drips slowly through the filter (picture 14). The result is highly aromatic and contains very few bitter compounds. The machine is also ideally suited for preparing tea and above all for creating alcoholic macerations (see p.125). My favourite is the brand Hario.

Dehydrator

A simple inexpensive dehydrator (picture 16) helps facilitate the production of "dusts" (see p.124) as well as ham and fruit "chips". Alternatively, you can use the oven.

Juices

When using juices you should always place great emphasis on freshness and quality. There are some simple rules of thumb that will more or less guarantee you can't go wrong: freshly pressed is superior to shop-bought juice; ripe fruits are better than unripe or frozen products; organic products beat fruits cultivated conventionally; and hand-pressing gives better results than electric devices. My recipes make do without exotic juices and limit themselves to the most commonly available varieties. For simplicity's sake, I resort to purchased products from good suppliers for coconut, tomato, and cranberry juices.

Juices

Freshly pressed

By "fresh" many bartenders really do mean pressed "à la minute", that is to say: from the fruit, into the drink. Since fresh juices oxidize and spoil rapidly this approach is of course the right one. Having said that, studies have shown that lime juice, for example, doesn't reach peak quality until 3–4 hours after pressing.

Using prepared juices

I want to give you a clear conscience if you press your juices for your guests shortly before they arrive and store them in clean bottles to use throughout the evening. That's exactly what we do at the Golden Bar, too. At the end of the evening, however, the juices really will have gone past their best and shouldn't be used beyond this time, with the exception of grapefruit juice, which keeps for 3–4 days without any problem. If you have prepared too much juice, you can freeze it and use it again at a later date. To pep up defrosted citrus juices, take the peel from some fresh fruits (as far as possible without the white pith under the skin), warm it up in a saucepan with some water, and then squeeze out the essential oils over the juice. You can also use this method to make fresh juices even more aromatic as all citrus juices are enhanced by their essential oils.

Citrus juices

Limes, lemons, oranges, and grapefruit are best juiced using a hand press. Only use an electric juicer if you require large quantities.

Apple, pineapple, ginger

You can't use a hand press to produce juices from apples, pineapples, or ginger. They are easy to make using a juicer (centrifuge), even in large quantities.

Cranberry, tomato, coconut water

These juices, as explained earlier, are best bought from a good supplier, which is perfectly acceptable.

There's hardly a drink that can be made without sugar in one form or another. You can even set yourself a rule of thumb that a little dash of sugar syrup will enhance virtually any drink – just like the renowned pinch of salt when cooking. Using artificial sweeteners completely goes against my philosophy. Sugar is a flavour carrier whereas sweeteners are always accompanied by unpleasant background flavours. It is so much better to use proper sugar and to do so consciously, rather than let yourself be tempted down the path of using sugar substitutes, only to end up consuming more calories than you actually intended. The herbal sweetener, Stevia, can be an interesting sweetener for some tea blends, but you really need to be partial to the liquorice-like aftertaste. Agave syrup is better tolerated by diabetics, but still needs to be consumed in moderation. Deciding which sugar to use depends on your own taste as well as the type of drink or syrup you are going to use the sugar in.

Sugar and syrup

Sugar and Syrup

White sugar

This is the most neutral tasting of all the sugars. Since it has a pure sweetness and doesn't distort the result with any ancillary flavours, it is perfect for producing simple sugar syrup and other recipes that require sugar. White sugar consists of sucrose, which is refined from sugar beet or sugar cane. The resulting juice is boiled and centrifuged to produce crystalline raw sugar, which must then be bleached, usually using chemicals.

Brown sugar

This is just as laborious to produce as white sugar and is then coloured using molasses.

Muscovado sugar

During normal sugar production the crystals are separated with the help of a centrifuge; when making muscovado sugar on the other hand, the boiled sugar cane juice is dried until it crystallizes. By pre-treating it in different ways, you get light or dark sugar. The dark variety has a very strong flavour of molasses, while the appeal of the lighter variant lies in its delicate treacle notes, which is why I love to use the latter in some of my recipes. Above all, light muscovado sugar gives syrups a lovely depth. In addition it has the highest proportion of vitamins and minerals of all the sugar varieties.

Unrefined sugar/ demerara sugar

Unrefined sugar is manufactured in the same way as white sugar, but isn't refined at the end. That means it isn't white and it naturally possesses a proportion of molasses, which give it a stronger and more full-bodied flavour. Demerara sugar is a typical unrefined sugar. I recommend using it in drinks and syrups where you want a bit more depth and breadth.

Molasses

These are the blackish-brown sugar cane juices that result from processing the sugar cane. They are often used in baking in the UK and are the raw material for all rums made from fresh sugar cane juice, except for the cane juice rums (Rhum agricole). You will need to use molasses very cautiously when mixing drinks as they have an extremely intense and distinctive flavour.

Organic sugar

This is primarily distinguished by the fact that the refined sugar is not allowed to be bleached chemically at the end of processing. From a flavour perspective, due to the residual proportion of molasses, it lies somewhere between unrefined sugar and white sugar.

Honey

This is a natural sweetener that imparts a huge variety of flavours and sweetness depending on the type of flower and its origin. It is essential for recipes where its distinctive full flavour plays a major role. Runny honey is discussed on page 123. A little spritz of this rounds off many drinks.

Agave syrup/agave juice concentrate

This liquid form of sugar works particularly well in drinks with mezcal or tequila because they are produced from the same raw material: the agave. Agave syrup became known among bartenders through Julio Bermejo from Tommy's Bar in Los Angeles who used it in Tommy's Margarita. The aroma is sometimes slightly grassy, the sweetness is stronger than in normal sugar syrup thanks to the higher proportion of fructose, and the syrup is less viscose on the tongue.

Syrups

In the Basic Recipes section (see pp.120–125) you will find recipes for all the syrups used in the book, from the simple sugar syrup (simple syrup) to highly aromatic varieties based on fruits, tea, or malt beer. Making your own syrups might be somewhat more time-consuming, but it is fun and gives you an opportunity to create flavours that can't be bought in any shop, especially if you use modern preparation techniques such as sous vide, pressure infusion, or the freezer method, all of which I describe in the Appendix. Making a syrup really is worth the effort, not least because the quality, even on your first attempts, will be far better than in any purchased product, although of course you can always use these, too.

My tip

Play around with a recipe using different sources of sugar to experience the important role played by each.

Ice

Ice is one of the most important factors for a good drink. When I talk about solid ice in my recipes, I mean large, clear, full ice cubes with edges around 3cm (1in) long. Little cones with a hole, nuggets, or shards are a no-no. And make sure that everything is prepared with the utmost cleanliness at each stage of the process!

Ice cubes

To make these professionally, you ideally need filtered water and rectangular silicon moulds from a good kitchen stockist. Fill the moulds, then place in a tray filled with water, so that the water just covers the moulds, and freeze. Once frozen carefully free the ice moulds from the frozen block, chipping away the excess ice from the edges. Remove the ice cubes from the silicon moulds. This produces double-frozen ice, which is used in many of the top bars. This method is ideal for ice added to stirred drinks, which should be kept extremely cold and require very little "melt" water. For domestic use, bags of ice are also widely available. Or you can ask a nearby bar, who may be happy to top up your supplies now and then in exchange for an appropriate tip. Anyone who wishes to acquire an ice-making machine for a professional bar should consider getting one size bigger than they estimate they need to ensure they will have sufficient ice.

Crushed ice

The best crushed ice is made by taking double frozen ice cubes and crushing them in an ice crusher or Thermomix before subsequently freezing them again, stirring them up repeatedly while they are freezing. The result is a fine granularity with optimum cooling characteristics. Alternatively, you can crush the ice cubes in a clean linen bag using a wooden hammer or similar.

Ice blocks and ice chunks

For self-hewn ice you need a clear block of ice, which you can order from an ice supplier, or the internet. I have a preference for using large chunks of ice that have been chipped off an ice block. If you want to make your own clear block of ice, fill a Thermobox of the required size with distilled or filtered water and place this without a lid in the freezer. The ice block will freeze through from top to bottom until it is crystal clear, apart from a dull strip on the base, which you will need to chip off using an ice saw or ice pick.

Ice balls

Ice balls are usually carved by hand, but to make these at home I use water bomb balloons. Fill the balloons with filtered water, tie them, and place them in the freezer so that they lie more or less spherically. This method results in slightly cloudy balls, but the advantage is you have hygienic individual packaging which is easy to handle.

Preparation: Shaken, Stirred...

With the appropriate equipment and a couple of simple steps you can mix up practically any drink. Only the shaker requires a bit of practice. The photos on the following pages show you how to handle the most important tools and ingredients.

1 Shaken

Place the ingredients in the shaker with ice for a wet shake, or without ice for a dry shake, close the lid, and shake vigorously for 10–15 seconds. By shaking with ice the drink not only gets chilled, but also some melt water is transferred into the drink – how much of this you want depends on the type of drink. After around 90 seconds, the drink won't get any colder and it will hardly absorb any more melt water. To practice, you can half fill the shaker with uncooked grains of rice, which has a similar feel to shaking with drink ingredients and ice.

2 Stirred

As a rule, all the ingredients for a drink are stirred together for 10–15 seconds in a mixing glass. While stirring for longer will make the drink colder, it also dilutes it more; something which is actually desirable in certain drinks. After around 90 seconds, just as with shaking, the drink won't change much more.

3 Built in the glass

This is how we describe mixing together and stirring all the ingredients on ice in the customer's glass. Cocktails such as the Old Fashioned, Rasta Nail, and all long drinks, such as the Moscow Mule, for example, are built up in the glass.

4 Prepared in the bottle

Some drinks can be prepared and kept cool until your guests arrive. These drinks are therefore ideal for larger gatherings or parties. Preparing something ahead in the bottle is nothing to be ashamed of: as far back as 150 years ago, professional bartenders were using this technique to help cope with sudden peaks in demand. Not only do you save time this way, but also every drink is of the same quality because the recipe is accurately measured out only once. Simply take the specified quantity of ingredients for the recipe and multiply by the number of guests, mix it all up in a larger container, decant into clean bottles, and store in the fridge. Before use, shake briefly and carry out any additional steps according to the recipe. To compensate for the lack of melt water, you should add a splash of water to clear bottled drinks.

Whether you use a Hawthorne or a julep strainer, the main concern is that only the ingredients that ultimately belong in the drink actually end up in the glass. The origin of the julep strainer dates back to when people would have used a strainer while drinking a classic julep cocktail, placing it on the cup to avoid swallowing little bits of ice or mint.

5 Straining or filtering

This has to be done for almost all drinks that are prepared in a shaker or mixing glass. Hold the strainer at the opening of the shaker or mixing glass and pour the drink through the sieve into the drinking glass.

6 Double straining or fine filtering

These are the terms used for straining drinks to filter out any tiny pieces of ice, fruit, or herbs that don't belong in the drinking glass. To do this, a little tea strainer is held between the strainer and the glass.

7 & 8 Squeezing citrus zest

Thinly slice a piece of peel from your citrus fruit and squeeze it over the drink. Citrus zest will imbue the drink with a wonderful aroma, but the remaining peel shouldn't be added to the drink because it contains a lot of bitter substances that will flavour the drink too strongly. Exceptions to this rule are recipes where precisely this effect is desired. In these cases, care should be taken that the zest is free of any white pith because this is particularly bitter.

Squeeze (no picture)

If a squeeze is required, take a little slice of citrus fruit, for example, one-sixth of a lime, squeeze this over the drink, and then add the slice to the drink.

Crusta (no picture)

To create a "crusta" (sugared rim), moisten the edge of the glass and dip it into a plate covered with sugar – how deep and for how long depends on the desired width and hardness of the crusta. Countless varieties of crusta can be made using different sugars and liquids. A particularly fine crusta can be made by spraying the top of the glass with the appropriate liqueur from an atomizer and then turning it in sugar or powder to coat.

The author (pages 4-95)

ERIC GROSSMAN
Eric Grossman is a spirits, dining, and travel
writer based in Boston and New Orleans, USA.
He writes extensively about craft spirits and
international cocktail trends, most notably for *USA
Today.* He has visited numerous distilleries and
judged cocktail competitions. Always eager to
share his knowledge, Eric is a true ambassador for
the craft spirits industry and is viewed as a "key
influencer" by several liquor companies and
branding agencies.
EHGrossman.com

Author's thanks

Brian Barrio, Tom Brady, Sharon Coppel, Scott
Gastel, Chris Godleman, Armida Gonzalez, Ellen
Grossman, Jeffrey Grossman, Grossman Family,
Hayflick Family, Informed Diner supporters, Janne
Johansson, Gerrish Lopez, Otto Lopez, Lopez
Family, TK Gore, James Jackson, Jimmy Lynn,
Chris Martin, Patrick McGee, Cheryl Patsavos,
Alex Pember, Jim Raras, Brandon Ross, Richard
Royce, Adam Salter, John Tierney, the entire DK
team, and the world's finest producers, distillers,
bartenders, and experts for their valued assistance.

The author & the photographer (pages 96-141)

KLAUS ST. RAINER is one of the best known and most successful bartenders in Germany. He has been involved in gastronomy since 1986 and worked for five years as head barman for Ernst Lechthaler before he transferred over to the legendary Schumann's Bar in Munich for seven years. In 2010 he opened the Golden Bar in Munich's Haus der Kunst together with Leonie von Carnap. In 2012 he was awarded "Bartender of the Year" at the Mixology Bar Awards, and in 2013 his bar achieved the distinction of "Bar of the Year". The British magazine Drinks International rated the Golden Bar one of the "Top 50 Bars of the World". Klaus St. Rainer is an adjudicator in many international competitions and runs training sessions all around the world. In addition, he is a co-founder of the Munich Bar Circle (Barzirkel München), proprietor of a cocktail shaker manufacturer, and sells his own bitters and tonic water.

WWW.GOLDENEBAR.DE

ARMIN SMAILOVIC is one of the most prestigious portrait photographers and photojournalists in Germany. Since 1995 he has worked as a freelance photographer around the globe for German and international magazines. He has won multiple awards. Among other things he won the LEAD Award's 2010 "best coverage of the year" and 2013 "best portrait photography of the year" and in 2014 received the highly regarded Hansel Mieth prize. Since 2010 he has been a founding member of the Munich FotoDoks festival for documentary photography. He lives in Munich and Sarajevo.

Author's thanks

Thank you to Leonie and my family, in which I also include my Screw Crew: Oliver von Carnap, Maximilian Hildebrandt, Claudius Kramer Brudnjak, Robbie Flörke, Jenny Lang, Mirko Hecktor, Julia Nather, Wicked, Ali, Anton Utin, Julian Zerressen, Dennis Richter, Chrissla Rieder, Messi Messerklinger, Ervin Mesanovic, Arpad Nikhazi, Axa Hötzinger, Ina Chil Soon Leuther, Wilfried Scherbinek, Christian Kaul, Jürgen Wiese, Julian Kerkoff, Gsölli Gsöllpointner, Giaco Giambo and all the other fine people who have worked and continue to work with us. Particular thanks must also go Julia Otterbach and my close friend Armin Smailovic for their fantastic collaboration on this book.

DK would like to thank:

Photography: William Reavell.
Photography art direction: Vicky Read.
Recipe styling: Kate Wesson.
Prop styling: Linda Berlin.
Cocktail consultancy: Ed Thorpe.
UK spirits consultant: Mark Ridgwell.
Proofreading: Claire Cross.
Indexing: Vanessa Bird.

Picture credits

The publisher would like to thank all of the distilleries featured in the book for their kind permission to reproduce photographs. Thanks also to: **47 McHenry & Sons**: Peter Jarvis.

All other images © Dorling Kindersley
For further information see: **www.dkimages.com**